Our Time

Embracing the 21st Century
And a New Millennium

Observations of Our World
In a Time of Change

by
Melvyn N. Klein

Some Comments from Readers regarding the newspaper columns written by Melvyn N. Klein in the *Corpus Christi Caller-Times* newspaper from 1980 to Present

Mel Klein writes with sensitivity and understanding of the issues and foibles of our time. His humanity and common sense make his insights a 'must' read.

Dan W. Lufkin – Co-Founder,
Donaldson, Lufkin & Jenrette

These essays exhibit extraordinary breadth and depth: breadth in the wide range of interests and issues which engage Mel Klein; and depth in the insights and hidden truths he finds in people and events, great and little known.

Robert G. McKelvey – Executive Committee
Association of Rhodes Scholars

Your sensitive, strong, compelling leadership echoes throughout your superb writing.

Ben Love – Texas banking and business legend

You write extraordinarily well and your perspective is very thoughtful.

Jay A. Pritzker, Esq.

I am glad that you speak out on issues and value your views and your writing.

Henry Kravis – Founder
Kohlberg, Kravis & Roberts

I enjoy all of your articles...You are gifted as a writer and more important...you are a great American.

George L. Argyros – Chairman
Horatio Alger Association of Distinguished Americans, Inc.

...beautiful and insightful writing...

Red McCombs – Owner
Minnesota Vikings

Mel Klein's columns are a delight to read as they are thoughful, insightful, and bring a fresh perspective to the topic. I always look forward in anticipation to the next.

Robert Furgason
President, Texas A&M University-Corpus Christi

Your articles make my day.

W. A. (Tex) Moncrief, Jr.

You are able to crystallize thoughts that very few others are able to do.

Arthur Levitt, Jr. – Chairman
Securities & Exchange Commission

...unusually thoughtful...

Newton Minow – Former Chairman
Federal Communications Commission

I heartily endorse your brilliant, articulate sentiments.

John L. Loeb, Jr. – Former Ambassador to Denmark

Mel Klein is my most outstanding student in a lifetime of teaching Political Science. He thinks as a man of action and acts as a man of thought, and this unique combination is brilliantly reflected in his writings.

Dr. John G. Stoessinger – Cox Distinguished Professor of International Affairs, Trinity University
Formerly of Columbia University, International Fellows Program

It's fully appropriate that Mel Klein's timely comments in the Corpus Christi Caller-Times are codified in book form and made available for review beyond the Gulf Coast....definitely worth adding to one's collection of reflections on the closing decades of the century.

Sidney J. Sheinberg – Former President, MCA, Inc.
Original mentor of Steven Spielberg

Mel Klein's columns, read together in a sitting, show a remarkable breadth and freshness - how impressive to find a columnist whose 'spin' is not predictable!

Eleanor Butt Crook

Your article is very well written and honestly reflects the events that we shared in common.

Hubert H. Humphrey III – Former Attorney General
The State of Minnesota

...a fine job in bringing the public's attention to important issues.

Richard N. Conolly

...super writing.

Harvey Terrell – Former Chairman
The First National Bank of Birmingham;
Member, Southern Tennis Hall of Fame

I fully agree with your views. You have expressed them well.

Oded Aboodi – Former Time-Warner Key Advisor

I've read and enjoyed every one of your editorials - but you'll be hard to outdo the last one. I can sense a lot of insight into the character of the author (re: "Spring is a good time to examine the priorities in your life.")

Dr. Charles S. Clark, Sr.

...fine writings.
Ted Collins, Jr. – Midland, Texas

I always look forward to reading your articles.
Berdon Lawrence – Houston, Texas

Your column caused me to pause for a moment of introspection. Thanks for helping me reconsider how I am spending my time.
John T. Casey – Former President
American Medical International

I always read your Feedback columns and find them not only interesting but beautifully written.
Dorothy Kucera

...good articles - enjoy reading them... well done.
Charles Butt – San Antonio, Texas

Your insightful column said it all wonderfully.
Neil R. Grabois – Former President
Colgate University

Gee, if I'd have known you were a writer, too, I would have been more careful in your company.
John Updike, author

Your article is wonderful - an extraordinary contribution of journalism.
Reverend Robert Schuller

Your writing, leadership, and insights are valuable to us all.

Dan Bayley – Managing Director, Head of Investment Banking
Merrill Lynch

Your articles are most inspiring.

Dr. Burton E. Grossman – San Antonio, Texas

Thank you for expressing it so well.
I share your values - faith, family, and friends; that is what life is all about.

Bill Greehey – Chairman, CEO
Valero Energy Corporation

...wonderful articles.

James D. Woods – Former Chairman & CEO
Baker-Hughes

...enjoy your newspaper columns.

Marc Shapiro – Vice Chairman
Chase Manhattan Corporation

...very well written.

Jeff Sandefer – Austin, Texas

...superb.

Former British Prime Minister Margaret Thatcher
(regarding Mr. Klein's introduction of her)

...values, such as loyalty, honesty, and telling the truth, never change, and affect all areas of our life both professional and personal.

Jack H. Brown – Chairman, CEO
Stater Bros. Markets

As always, I enjoy reading your editorials.

Thomas S. Haggai – Chairman & CEO of IGA

As usual the piece was thoughtful and a pleasure to read.

Anne M. McSweeney
Special Advisor to the President of Columbia University

I thoroughly enjoyed reading your article about Jay (Pritzker).

Penny Pritzker

To My Good Friend, Mel Klein, whose insights and writings have helped me in my perspectives on life. I am excited to see Mel publishing this book because it focuses on what is truly valuable and important in life.

All of Mel's insights come from his core values, and it is these perspectives that make his writings so relevant in today's world.

Peter M. Holt – Chairman
Holt Companies and The San Antonio Spurs

Dad, we read a copy of your column today; it was good.

Jacqueline and Jenna Klein

A Texas A&M University/ Corpus Christi Publication.

Published by Woolford Publishing.
Book Jacket Cover design by Jim Forsythe.
Cover Photo of Mr. Klein by Thomas Jason of Fort Lauderdale, Florida.

Inquiries should be addressed to Permissions Department, Woolford Publishing / Melvyn N. Klein, 615 N. Upper Broadway, Corpus Christi, Texas 78477.

Library of Congress Cataloging-in-Publication Data

Klein, Melvyn N.
Our Time: Embracing the 21st Century and the New Millennium/
Melvyn N. Klein
ISBN 0-9675800-0-5

Printed in the United States of America

First Edition

Dedication

I dedicate this book to the three generations that helped shape "My Time."

To my mother and father, Bertha and Harry Klein, for instilling in me the strong roots of ethics and values – like hard work, honesty, loyalty, and service. The cornerstone of my achievements and legacy I credit to their character, sacrifice, and nurturing.

To my sister Elaine and her immediate family - Lane, Jeff, Alisa, and Cary, and my brother Marty for their steadfast confidence and encouragement.

To my wife, Annette, who stood by me during those growthful years when I reached for the stars.

And to my children, Jenna and Jacqueline, who carry forth into destiny the seed of my hopes and dreams for a new millennium.

Acknowledgements

Thank you to the many people who encouraged my writing of these editorial columns for the *Corpus Christi Caller-Times* newspaper and who requested their compilation into this book, and to the many readers who responded with their comments and actions during these 20 years.

I would like to thank . . .

Edward H. Harte, publisher of the *Corpus Christi Caller-Times* and his successor Steve Sullivan for the opportunity to write a regular column from 1980 through today.

The *Caller-Times* board of editors.....for their guidance.....especially to the editorial page editors with whom I had the pleasure of working and visiting throughout these years; they were exceptionally talented journalists - John L. Stallings, Jerry Norman, and Nick Jiminez.

My administrative assistant, Susan Barham, for her invaluable help in organizing and preparing these columns.

My editor and publisher, Jeff Woolford, for his editorial assistance, suggestions, and project management during the publication of this book.

My former law school roommate, Bob McKelvey of Sea Girt, New Jersey, for his commentary and insight on many early drafts of these columns - and his great friendship.

And those many people who were gracious enough to respond to my editorial columns with their comments and observations.

Table of Contents

Foreword

Edward H. Harte - Former Publisher, Corpus Christi Caller-Times

It is a fortunate occurrence that the columns which Mel Klein contributed over 20 years to the Corpus Christi Caller-Times are being saved in this permanent form. Like all daily journalism, they deal with events of the moment. But they deserve preservation for their broader dimension beyond the transitory concerns of the past.

Mel was one of several South Texans who were invited to write a periodic column for the paper's Op-Ed department, "Feedback." Of that stable of writers, which included notables in the area like Anne Armstrong and John Cypher, the biographer of Robert J. Kleberg, Jr., none wrote for as many years as Mel.

Mel brought to the task a reflective mind, honed in a number of disciplines, and informed by associations in the highest reaches of business and politics. His comments on events profited from that rich background — from investment banker, entrepreneur, and venture capitalist, to a political activist and university adjunct professor.

Several themes recur in these columns. Mel often sees events as reflections of individual courage or enterprise, and propounds his view that individuals can and do make a difference. He finds lessons in the past, but his preoccupation is with the future, the accelerating pace of change and the challenges it presents.

He is deeply interested in the young and often writes about them in a sympathetic vein. He is a zealous, if unself-conscious, patriot and he uses his column to promote basic values which he thinks can assure the continuation of American leadership.

Mel took the writing of these columns seriously. He had no staff to do research and often had to dig out and verify "facts" himself. Like most newspaper columnists, he confessed to moments of writer's block. And like most newspaper columnists, he wanted his essays to be read and discussed.

They were read and discussed, for reasons that will be clear as you read on.

Special Comment

Former President George H. W. Bush:

I have read a number of your columns and have enjoyed your insights and commentary on people and issues of importance during the past twenty years. Your article on our great M.D. Anderson Cancer Center and your reference to it in another column are consistent with the dedication to the Anderson that we share. It is the world's leader in cancer treatment and research and is in the forefront of finding a cure for cancer. I look forward to continuing to work with you to advance this great hospital. I also look forward to having a copy of your book.

Introduction

Beginning in 1980, I was honored by being invited to write a regular guest editorial column for the *Corpus Christi Caller-Times* from then until now. I was given the freedom to select topics and express my own points of view.

Such an enlightened editorial policy is one of the many reasons that the *Corpus Christi Caller-Times* is such a respected newspaper. The *Corpus Christi Caller-Times* received extensive recognition as best daily newspaper in Texas, New Mexico, Oklahoma, Arkansas, and Louisiana in its category for eight of the last eleven years; it was runner-up the other three. The Press Club of Dallas sponsored the selection which was judged by the University of Missouri-Columbia journalism department.

My residence was in Corpus Christi Texas, throughout these years; my wife and I brought up and educated our two daughters until they left for college at Princeton and Stanford respectively. My business was based elsewhere throughout those years - New Orleans, Chicago, New York, Los Angeles, and other places. Accordingly, these are the writings of someone born in Chicago, reared in Indiana, schooled in upper state New York, New York City, Washington, D.C., and London, England, who wrote about the people and events of the time from a perspective not singularly rooted in any one place or region of the United States.

I endeavored to take my journalism responsibilities to heart and sought to bring to the reading public's attention those issues and newsmakers that impacted not only South Texas, but our country and our world. The subjects were selected for their relevance and importance to living during the last two decades of the twentieth century and the second millennium.

Many people encouraged and requested this compilation of columns and essays including those whose comments are quoted on the inside covers. Many of the columns received extensive feedback as having continuing significance. Some, frankly, have been shown by future developments to have lesser significance, such as "U.S. Produces the Best and Brightest, Like Ross Perot" (published September 27, 1986) and "Texas Should Keep an Eye on New Jersey's Governor's Race" (published August 19, 1989). All columns are reprinted here so that the reader has access to the totality of thought - on the mark or off.

Some columns were exceptionally prophetic and offered accurate insight into future happenings of consequence. One of the best examples of that was the column "Policymakers Need to Stand Back, and Take the Long View" (published October 29, 1988), which was jointly authored by my friend and business partner Tom Pritzker and myself. It was subsequently substantially re-printed in the *Chicago Tribune.* It was one of the very earliest publicly-articulated commentaries to predict and anticipate the primacy of economic competition rather than military confrontation among Cold War adversaries. Its significance was recognized by the Honorable Stuart E. Eizenstat, who wrote as follows:

> *There is an enormous amount of accumulated wisdom in this compilation of Mel Klein's newspaper columns. One especially prescient one in 1988 forecast the end of Communism in the Soviet Union. His were among the first writings which foretold the dramatic shifts from military priorities to economic relationships which would occur from this cataclysmic event in our relations with Russia, as well as ways our relationships with Europe, Japan, India, and Pakistan would be affected.*

These columns reflect the personal perspective of someone rooted in South Texas who traveled extensively and was directly involved in some of the events shaping this time. Many of the first drafts of these columns were written in an airplane. This book reflects one man's journey through these years as a businessman, attorney, father, husband, and teacher. It focuses upon issues - personal and public - and upon people that made a difference in shaping what was happening during our time.

The following essays provide a personal view of the major issues of our time from a unique perspective. This compilation is being published to allow contemporary consideration of the subjects covered and to provide a resource for future generations to better understand our time.

Mr. Melvyn N. Klein was honored as a Horatio Alger Award winner in 1996.

The following biography was originally published in the 1996 edition of Only in America *by the Horatio Alger Association of Alexandria, Virginia and is reprinted here with their permission.*

Melvyn N. Klein
President and Chief Executive Officer
JAKK Holding Corporation

"Think about our values and priorities and compare them to the actual ways we spend our time - remember what is most important - those whom we love, the wonder of nature and learning, and the greater purpose of our lives."

"Endless opportunities and a sense of unfulfilled destiny drive me," says Mel Klein, who knew at an early age that a career in just one field would not be enough to quench his thirst for doing as much as possible in one lifetime.

Klein is well known on Wall Street and in international financial circles. As president and chief executive officer of JAKK Holding Corporation, Klein co-founded and manages GKH Partners, L.P., with more than $500 million of equity capital, and is a founder and principal of $300 million Questor Partners, L.P. He is an attorney, an entrepreneur, a newspaper columnist, and the executive in residence and adjunct professor of business at Texas A&M University. In short, he has done what he set out to do. He is working simultaneously at the highest levels in areas that interest him - law, public service, business, entertainment, and education. A committed American, Klein freely gives his time, energy, and money to further the American dream for many, simply because he believes it is his responsibility. According to Klein, "Success is being able to give back to your country and community."

Klein is quick to credit his parents for his motivation and drive. "My father was a private hero for me. He was an ordinary person with extraordinary character who believed in the classical virtues." Growing up in the late 1940s and 1950s in Gary, Indiana, Klein was reared in a warm, nurturing environment. "My parents were hard-working people, dedicated to their family."

An electrician for U.S. Steel, Klein's father was often subject to strikes. "He sometimes worked shortened weeks," says Klein. "One summer my mother ran a tourist home because my father was out of work." During those times, Klein's father did whatever he could, even repairing lamps, to provide for his family. "I knew things were tough for my parents, so I learned to be economically self-sufficient at an early age." Klein had a paper route at age nine, which he worked seven days a week until he was 13. He then worked in the paper's circulation department, a job he held until his high school graduation.

Raised on the Horatio Alger stories, Klein was fascinated with the idea that hard work and determination could lead to the fulfillment of one's dreams. "I knew my family didn't have the financial advantages that would make it easy for me to achieve my goals, so I relied on myself to make it happen. Becoming self-reliant in childhood provides a quiet confidence and strength that grows and continues throughout your life."

Klein was a dedicated student and continues to be one to this day. "Those who think they have completed their education without building on it will not have full and complete lives," he says. Active in high school, Klein participated in debate, track, the school newspaper and student council. He graduated second in his class. He entered Colgate University in 1959 and worked his way through school as a messenger, waiter, salesman, and dishwasher. Klein also received financial assistance as a General Motors National Scholar.

Klein distinguished himself early at Colgate and was named chairman of the Freshman Honor Court. But tragedy struck during his freshman year. Klein was the only survivor of an automobile accident caused by a drunk driver. His debate partner and another close friend did not survive. "I had to ask myself, 'Why was I spared and they were not?' It made a deep impact on me and motivated me even more to make a positive impact with my life."

An able debater, Klein led his team to the New York state championship. As a member of Colgate's first economics study group, Klein studied at the London School of Economics and Political Science. He graduated from Colgate with highest honors in economics in 1963. In addition, he was named Outstanding Student in American Studies after he wrote his prize-winning paper, "On Our National Purpose," which led to his pursuit of a degree in law. Klein attended Columbia Law School and worked in the American International Group's General Counsel's office. Another honor came his way when he was named an International Fellow of Columbia University. "That allowed me to take courses in international affairs while I was in law school. I tried to pack 25 hours of living in every 24-hour day," he says. Klein also received the Edward John Noble Leadership Award, which provided a stipend toward the cost of law school.

Klein went to Washington, D.C. for a summer job with the law firm of Corcoran, Foley, Youngman and Rowe. "On my first day, Tommy Corcoran took me to the White House, which led to my being appointed to the National Executive Committee for Young Citizens for Johnson and Humphrey."

With his law degree in hand, Klein went to work as Congressman Yates' legislative assistant. In 1968, Vice President Humphrey asked Klein to help with his presidential bid. Later, Humphrey introduced Klein to the investment firm of Donaldson, Lufkin and Jenrette (DLJ). "I joined the firm in 1969 and helped build its investment banking business both domestically and internationally." Klein originated the idea of creating capital pools for principal investing. He first proposed the structure that was implemented and was instrumental in creating what became the Sprout Group. "Sprout I was one of the earliest direct equity investment funds for institutional investors and was a predecessor of the leveraged buyout funds," comments Dan Lufkin, one of DLJ's founders and a continuing partner of Klein. Klein's vision was among the earliest to transform an important part of the structure of America's free enterprise system. Klein became a senior vice president of the firm and served as director of DLJ Capital Corporation.

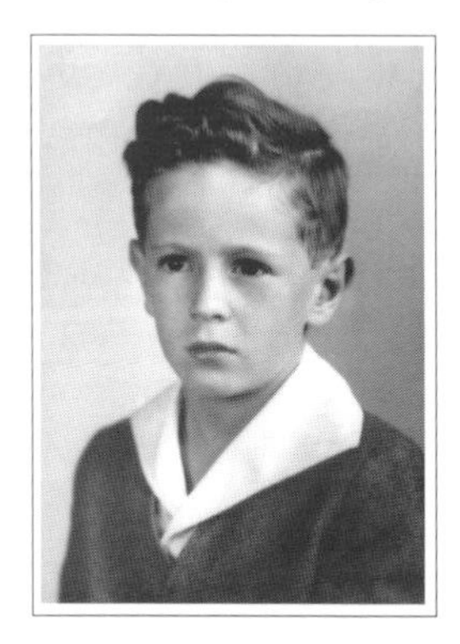
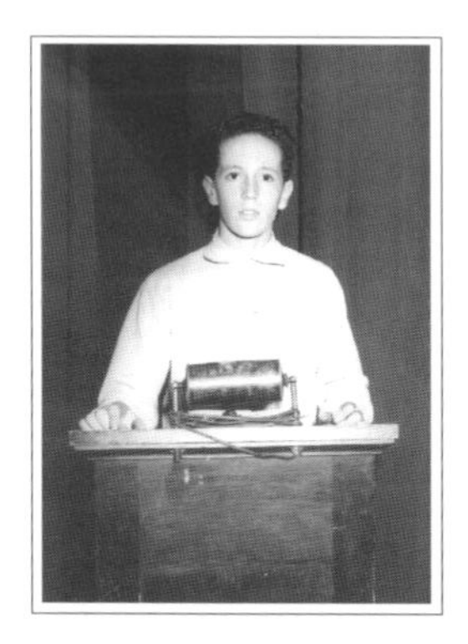

Klein was a debater in high school and went on to win debate championships in college.

In 1976, Klein married Annette Grossman and agreed to move to her hometown of Corpus Christi, Texas. "We wanted to bring up our children, Jacqueline and Jenna, amidst the surroundings and values that were consistent with the way we were raised," says Klein. "Our business interests are in New York, Los Angeles, Chicago, and other places, including internationally, but I make sure I'm not away from home for extended periods. I believe that parental dedication, as well as commitment to friends and fellow citizens, will sustain the values that keep us strong as individuals and as a country.

Since the mid-1970s, Klein has been involved in a number of entrepreneurial, investment, and management activities. He co-founded several energy companies that were built and sold successfully. He was chief executive officer of two listed public companies that were successfully built and merged - Altamil Corp. and Eskey, Inc. He co-founded two independent entertainment companies that produced or distributed feature films including *Sophie's Choice, The Fugitive, Shadowlands,* and *Circle of Friends.* He has served on the boards of directors and executive committees of a number of companies, including Anixter International, Levitz Furniture Corporation, Playboy Enterprises, Inc., American Medical International, Inc., Cockrell Oil and Gas, L.P., and Santa Fe Energy Resources, Inc.

In 1988, Klein organized a $550 million equity investment partnership, GKH Partners, L.P. "We are distinctive with the extent to which we become knowledgeable and involved with the companies in which we invest," says Klein. He has served as its managing general partner since its inception.

GKH became a part of several of history's biggest takeover battles in the 1980s, including the $25 billion fight for RJR Nabisco. Klein was one of those who led the partnership's successful leveraged buyout of American Medical International, Inc., for $3.5 billion. It was the last major leveraged buyout of the era. The company was sold in March 1995 with nearly $2 billion of equity value created in six years. Klein serves on the board of each GKH investment.

To say Klein is busy with a range of activities is clearly an understatement. "My motivation to contribute has come from a combination of values learned from my parents, certain teachers in my life, and the accident I was in during college. These experiences reinforced my desire to make the most out of my life."

Apart from business and public service, Klein has served as a regular guest editorial writer for the *Corpus Christi Caller-Times* since 1980. He writes on a variety of subjects including the character of true heroes and the distinction between genuine heroes and celebrities. He also writes about public policy issues, personal growth, the free enterprise system, and classic values.

After giving a commencement speech last year at Texas A&M in Corpus Christi, Klein was invited by the university's president to be the university's first executive in residence. In that role, he has addressed different subjects - environmental issues, organizational behavior, and trends that will impact his students in the coming century. Currently, he is teaching a weekly seminar on entrepreneurship. "I'm glad to give something back to these young people. I owe a lot to certain teachers who influenced and enhanced my life."

His Horatio Alger Award has special meaning for Klein. "My father was an admirer of the Horatio Alger stories. When he was terminally ill with cancer in 1988, I had an opportunity to attend the Horatio Alger Awards ceremony. When I returned, I shared the program book with my father. We discussed the evening in great detail. He was emotionally and deeply affected by the accomplishments of the Awardees and the work of the Association in terms of encouraging and helping young people proceed with their lives. He viewed the Horatio Alger Award as the highest recognition of an earned life of consequence. I agree with my father's high opinion. I am deeply honored to be part of a group of people I have admired all my life."

Klein gives time and resources to a wide range of activities, including the M.D. Anderson Cancer Center at the University of Texas, the Art Museum of South Texas, and a long list of charitable organizations. He was a member of

Klein was a member of the national campaign staff when Hubert Humphrey ran for President.

Appointed by President Reagan to the Grace Commission, Klein greets the President during a White House reception.

the Young Presidents' Organization and is a current member of the World Presidents' Organization. He addresses many leadership classes in Texas and elsewhere. When it comes to mentoring, Klein recalls his father once again. "My father gave little advice in his life. When he did, his message was simple: At the end of life, few people wish they had spent more time worrying, criticizing, or being negative. Be positive and don't lose perspective about what really matters."

Mel Klein's parents, Bertha and Harry Klein.

Mel and Annette Klein have two daughters, Jenna (a sophomore at Stanford University) and Jacqueline (an actress in Los Angeles).

Texas A & M University (Corpus Christi) President Robert Furgason joins the Klein family prior to Klein's commencement address.

Tom Pritzker (left), Mel Klein, Arnold Schwarzenegger, and Jay Pritzker at Planet Hollywood opening. The Pritzkers have been Klein's business partners for more than 25 years.

Klein visits with President George Bush, Commerce Secretary Robert Mosbacher, and Robert Chilton during the American Business Conference.

"Texan Mel Klein nation's quiet, heavy-hitting investor."
Quote from Associated Press

Klein with baseball great Nolan Ryan and Jim Peterson, former chairman of the National Restaurant Association. Klein served as master of ceremonies for a charitable event to benefit the M.D. Anderson Cancer Center

Klein attends a party with Dan Lufkin and others from Donaldson, Lufkin and Jenrette.

Section I

People of South Texas

We're Lucky To Live Here

(Published December 26, 1981)

When I began to consider possible subjects for this column, several global and cosmic ones came to mind. They included (1) an expression of confidence that our recently-effective national economic recovery program will be successful and will be perceived as such during next year, (2) observations about President Reagan's first year in office, and (3) the fact that the continuing bad news of 1981 will end in five days.

After those initial ideas, my thoughts turned to the question of what could be written that would express feelings consistent with those of the beautiful moments, the cherished memories, and the warmth of family and friends during this holiday season. The subject that seemed appropriate for today is the expression of how fortunate we are to live in this great, free country: the problems and confusion in many places around the world provide real perspective.

We are, indeed, even more fortunate that we live here in South Texas.

This is my fifth year as a resident of Corpus Christi. The pioneer families, and those that followed, who built this increasingly cosmopolitan city are owed a debt of gratitude by those who have moved here more recently. Having lived in a number of other places in this country and overseas, I have a special regard for the quality of life and for the standards that prevail in this community.

We have a stable and growing economy that is led by businesses involved in agriculture, energy, tourism, and marine transportation. The renaissance that is taking place downtown reflects vision and good leadership; the new buildings, planned and completed, are improving our skyline and enhancing Corpus Christi's image. While this city is undergoing significant change, it doesn't threaten deep-seated traditions; Buccaneer Days and Bayfest continue to be enjoyable for all who are involved.

Anyone who has not attended a performance at the Bayfront Plaza, seen an exhibit at the Art Museum of South Texas, or participated in numerous events that enrich life here is missing a wonderful experience. While differences and controversies receive considerable attention in this multi-racial, multi-ethnic environment, we have, nonetheless, a strong, overriding sense of community life.

Even more important than our cultural climate and beautiful bayfront is the character of most people who live here. An atmosphere of community commitment and caring exists that has been reflected in the United Way campaign and the community's response to the recent theft at the Salvation Army. The "ostrich" impulse is rarely found as men and women - and boys and girls - participate through a multitude of organizations, or as individuals, in a broad range of projects and institutions that continuously expand the horizons of community life - and seek to do more.

With its physical assets and human resources, South Texas is ready for the challenge of the coming new year. The promise of 1982 and beyond is truly a positive and exciting one.

Homeport Is Already Paying Off

(Published September 7, 1985)

"I think, that as life is action and passion, it is required of a man that he should share the passion and action of his time, at peril of being judged not to have lived."
- Oliver Wendell Holmes

For one year, much of the action and passion of life for men and women in our South Texas community has been related to economic development and, specifically, to Homeport. In early September of 1984, the Corpus Christi Chamber of Commerce organized and led a team to respond to the late August request by the Navy to submit a bid for a Gulf Coast homeport.

The successful result is now history. The process itself, as well as the tremendous accomplishment, had a major impact on this area. As South Texas Homeport task force chairman Loyd Neal recently wrote, "Everyone in the Coastal Bend came together to dream and work together towards the realization of one goal . . . "

This task force will remain in place until Homeport receives its ships, necessitated by the uncertain policy and political dynamics of the federal government's budgets. Although the crucial funding legislation for Homeport isn't scheduled to be included in the federal budget until fiscal 1988, master plan development and environmental impact studies by the Navy are scheduled to begin this fall.

While we may have to wait a few years for Homeport, the Corpus Christi area has realized at least three major benefits already.

First, a new confidence has emerged and is being expressed. Anticipatory and preparatory investment commitments have been made and many others are expected. Homeport potential, combined with lower interest rates and other factors, has improved residential and commercial real estate values. A surging entrepreneurial spirit has evolved. The mind-set of innovation, commitment, and hard work that led to Homeport is similar to that required for successful entrepreneurship. Entrepreneurs, often working closely with public officials, have begun to transform the shorelines and skylines.

Secondly, many people previously uninvolved have become very interested and committed to helping economic development activities during this past year. To ensure a sound economic base, a community needs the commitment of its citizenry, such as those who developed the Corpus Christi '90 report and those who contribute in countless other smaller or larger ways. As more people become involved, they generate ideas which can lead to job- and tax-generating business locating in this area. Many new prospects have recently been developed by broader knowledge of, and interest in, business development. Many people have contributed their talent and/or money to the effort; others have made planes or facilities available.

Thirdly, those organizations and institutions responsible for different aspects of economic development in Corpus Christi have markedly improved their coordination with one another. The Chamber of Commerce, the Tourist and Convention Bureau, the Business Development Commission and the Port Authority have implemented improved means of communication and operating together. In addition, Corpus Christi and its neighboring communities have developed closer working relationships in projects of mutual interest. For example, it was a joint Corpus Christi/Kingsville delegation that made the Saturn presentation to General Motors officials in Detroit a few months ago.

If you haven't yet shared in, or been part of "the passion and action" that is shaping this area as we move toward a new century, the second week of September 1985 is not too late to participate.

Strong Cultural, Business Foundation Needed For Progress

(Published April 26, 1986)

This is an important time for business and cultural development in Corpus Christi, and the two are closely linked. Businesses often locate where their people want to live, and cultural offerings are key factors in decision-making. Recent occurrences in both of these areas are presently converging to create an opportunity to significantly enhance this area's economic and cultural base.

The only executive director that the Business Development Commission has ever had resigned after 18 years of able service. Coincidentally, the BDC, the Chamber of Commerce, and city, county, and port officials have been reviewing the structure of the BDC in order to strengthen its effectiveness in the highly competitive world of attracting business and investment, and creating jobs. In order to increase its budget, coordinate programs with clear accountability for results, and broaden private support and involvement, Corpus Christi's BDC will soon undergo a constructive evolution.

Whatever personnel or structure changes occur, the quality of life in Corpus Christi, especially educational and cultural, will continue to be an important competitive edge for business development.

This community, with both public and private leadership and financial support, continues to improve upon what is available to those of us who live here and to those whom we seek to attract. Voters earlier this month approved bond financing for necessary infrastructure, and also to assist the Texas State Aquarium to come into being in this city. An endowment fund has recently been established to build the permanent collection of the Art Museum of South Texas. Groundbreaking for the water garden in Bayfront Arts and Science Park is planned for late summer. The successful completion of these projects will require continuing hard work and financial support.

Further, the Corpus Christi Museum expansion, library book purchase, the mercado, and other worthwhile projects that did not receive voter approval for public bond financing a few weeks ago would contribute to an educational and cultural environment that would enhance Corpus Christi. Other means need to be explored to make them happen - either public or private, or a combination of both.

A remarkable characteristic of this area is the depth of volunteer commitment. Whether it's preparing for tomorrow's Art Jamboree, or organizing symphony, theatrical, or ballet programs, many people do their share in contributing to our cultural life.

Even though this is a tough time for certain sectors of our economy, we must find a way to combine public and private resources to implement those projects that will strengthen our cultural base and assist those who will be responsible for business development.

Does Corpus Christi Want What Gambling Would Bring?

(Published September 5, 1987)

What sort of community is this? What do we want it to be?

An impressive group of our fellow citizens will soon be encouraging us to vote for legalized gambling in Texas, and, more specifically, for pari-mutual betting on dog racing in this county. While I respect many of the messengers, I reject the message and shall vote no on Nov. 3.

Among the noteworthy local endorsers, I am not aware of anyone who has actual experience in controlling and operating legalized gambling activity. I have had such experience and do not want the fact of, or the atmosphere of, legalized gambling anywhere near here.

My experience was in another part of the country where the population felt they had no alternative but to approve casino gambling to economically revive their city. We were assured that organized crime and significant spontaneous crime, could be contained. On certain levels that was true - but not completely, and that makes all the difference. Gambling is an invitation to crime; even proponents acknowledge the problem. While pari-mutual betting is perceived as "cleaner" than casino gaming, a gambling business is a gambling business!

Wherever cash flows freely in a gambling business on a large scale, you do not have to be a law enforcement expert, nor do you need to see "The Godfather" a second time to know that the community has taken a significant risk - with insufficient reward.

The argument that betting on dog races is good for economic development is hollow. While some tourists will be attracted, others will turn away. Dollars will flow from poorer people here who can least afford it to the developers and owners; dollars will be re-allocated within our community. Who really believes that we shall attract substantial high-rollers here to go to the dog races, when they can go to gambling pleasure spas that offer much more than dogs?

Our strength is the quality of life and the character and culture of the people who live here. We are distinctive in our family-oriented Bayfest, Buccaneer Week, sailing, fishing, and other sports. Our arts, theater, concert, and other entertainment capabilities are extensive and growing. The Bayfront Plaza/Heritage Park area will command world recognition as it continues to evolve. The Texas State Aquarium will soon be here. Legalized gambling in any form, much less betting on dog races, will detract from our quality of life and our city's image. It is inconsistent with all that makes this area special, and will not bring in the kind of tourist business that we want. San Antonio, Orlando, San Diego, and countless other places with standards similar to ours, and tourist businesses to nourish, have refused to permit gambling.

Further, exposing children to daily reinforcement that gambling is an approved activity does not build character. Parents and teachers have enough of a challenge instilling standards of responsibility, hard work, and sacrifice to add gambling to the addictions to be avoided.

The cruelty to animals that can occur while training for dog races would seem too obviously unacceptable as to merit no further comment.

The importance of the military to this area is also readily apparent - from the Naval Air Station to Homeport. Our community's culture is relevant to decision-makers in the armed services. Dog-race wagering will not enhance the bond that the military has with us.

Previous generations have given us a legacy of a great quality of life. It is hard to imagine that our values and goals for the future include betting on dog races. How many of us can be proud to be part of the generation that brought dog-race gambling to our community?

March Events Portend Great Promise For City's Future

(Published March 18, 1989)

Those who studied Latin, or the history of the Roman Empire, will be especially sensitive to this time of year. Mid-March, or the Ides of March, was a time during which a fortune-teller told Julius Caesar to be especially vigilant. He wasn't, and perished. Having been very impressionable when I first learned this bit of history, I have always been conscious of March as a month of potential special consequence. It has often been just that; for example, consider this month and its importance for Corpus Christi, and then decide whether this timing is a matter of coincidence - or significance.

On March 1, Dr. Henry Kissinger visited our city and began the month and his address by telling hundreds of supporters of Spohn Hospital's new radiation therapy center, "It's not the critics and skeptics who change the world. Great achievements begin as somebody's ideal. They are pursued, developed, and brought into being."

Soon thereafter, a Corpus Christi Economic Outlook conference was held which communicated a positive feeling for the future that anticipated stable progress. The ideal of our region moving toward economic strength received encouragement. The Texas Senate then took a specific step forward to making a four-year university a reality in Corpus Christi. Homeport and the Texas State Aquarium continue on course. This month is also important as the period immediately preceding city elections. Those who will guide Corpus Christi into the '90s as it prepares for a new century will be elected.

One of our most important organizations, Leadership Corpus Christi, conducted a program for its current class entitled "Corpus Christi - The Next Generation." It provided education and insight for another group of probable leaders and contributors to the growth and enhancement of this community. While problems were not minimized, opportunities and our area's "edges and advantages" were emphasized.

Two of our greatest edges and advantages are our quality of life and the physical beauty of this area. Many believe that the season to experience the best of South Texas is spring, which begins within days. Tens of thousands of young students - in fact or at heart - have been welcoming spring and celebrating in advance. As the beauty of spring returns to South Texas, the drawing power and attractiveness of life in this area is exceptional. Those working to bring new business, capital, and capable people to Corpus Christi will receive considerable support from the weather, the ambience, and the happenings of spring. All this begins in the month of March.

Further, this is an important time as almost 500 parents and other volunteers on the Corpus Christi Independent School District's strategic planning project teams work on completing their missions. The efforts currently being made have the potential and promise to improve many aspects of our primary and secondary school system. There are few matters of greater importance to a community than achieving excellence in the education of its children. Many innovations may be anticipated, including providing for "innovative funding from public and private sources," and implementing "a program to aggressively recruit and retain quality personnel."

Much has happened, and still will occur almost every day in March in many other matters of interest. On the final day of the month, Art in the Heart, which symbolizes and reinforces the renaissance of downtown, will begin.

In a different era and in another place, Caesar ignored the signs. We have very favorable prospects, even though we have many challenges and issues to address. Whether the Ides of March 1989 portend real progress and great achievements for South Texas can only be known with certainty in the future. To ensure the fulfillment of the destiny that is indicated, we should complete the unfinished, achieve consensus on other goals, be vigilant in meeting civic and community responsibilities, and remain committed to a positive course and attitude.

Corpus Christi, Barcelona Will Mark Columbus Anniversary

(Published April 21, 1990)

While viewing a sculpture honoring Christopher Columbus recently in Barcelona, Spain, two observations came to mind. One was the consciousness-raising opportunity created by the 1992 milestone of the fifth century of Columbus' discovery of the Americas. The other was how similar Barcelona was to Corpus Christi, age and size differences notwithstanding.

A 500-year anniversary is of such epic significance that a celebration, rather than a crisis, could provide the catalyst to bring forth those great qualities that discovered and then built this country. The kind of outstanding vision and leadership that led to America's discovery is needed in the 1990s.

An alienated public's opinion, diversions from challenging reality, and slipping standards have replaced leadership. We are not producing the ideas or the leaders needed to debate and define vital questions, much less resolve them and guide our state and nation to discover and implement answers to pressing problems.

A New World order began in 1492. With the stunning pace of events today, we are participating in another of history's moments of fundamental change. An opportunity exists to shape another New World order. While much has changed in the world in the 500 years since Columbus, one fact is as important today as it has been throughout history: one person can effect significant change.

Those essential qualities of leadership that can solve problems, create opportunities, and change the world remain vital - vision, courage, character, positive principles and purpose, and commitment. Of all the events and activities planned to celebrate Columbus' discovery, few could be as relevant as evoking the leadership and values that achieve great accomplishments which advance humanity. Our perspective can look forward as we look back in history.

Barcelona and Corpus Christi share the distinction of being two of the cities that will be most prominent in 1992 as centers of recognizing Columbus' great achievement. Barcelona is the city to which Columbus returned to announce his discovery of the New World. Barcelona is one of the two cities in Spain that will host an event international in scope as part of the Quincentenary festivities; Barcelona will host the 1992 Olympics. Corpus Christi has been designated the official Texas city for the Quincentenary celebration because of its historic relationship with Spain. Corpus Christi was discovered by another Spanish explorer, Alonzo de Pineda, and houses shipwreck artifacts from that era of discovery in the Corpus Christi Museum of Science and History. There is no question about the important Hispanic influence in our city.

A seacoast city, which is a regional center, that is an integral part of its state and nation, but has also been significantly influenced by a nearby foreign country, describes both Barcelona and Corpus Christi; the former is near France and the latter near Mexico. Each has a vital port and is a shipping, industrial, and educational center surrounded by agricultural communities. Each has a hardworking, generally optimistic, and religious population with much civic pride and a sense of its history. Each is relatively outside of mainstream activity and has developed unique strengths accordingly, including an excellent quality of life. Each is occasionally subject to rugged natural forces - Barcelona to flash flooding and Corpus Christi to hurricanes.

One other similarity is noteworthy. Barcelona and Corpus Christi are cities which emphasize the arts. Barcelona was fortunate to have been the home of one of the world's greatest architects/artists, Gaudi. His brilliant and innovative works are to be found throughout the city. His gardens, ceramic benches, buildings, parks, fantastic figures, and other secular and religious buildings, including the famous incomplete Church of the Sagrada Familia, enhance life and are a riveting attraction for the city. Accordingly, Barcelona is an excellent example of a city that attracts countless visitors because of its arts and architecture.

The Bayfront Arts and Science Park, Heritage Park, the Creative Arts Center, the Bayfront Art Center, and other aspects of Corpus Christi life reflect the importance placed upon the arts here. While we do not have a dominant artist like Gaudi, we have a diversity that is growing in scope and recognition. We need to support and encourage this dimension for our city and maintain its quality.

Port Must Defend, Preserve The Legacies Of Jimmie Storm

(Published July 20, 1991)

It may have been his quintessential South Texas upbringing. Perhaps it was his genes. It may have been the insight, wisdom and perspective acquired from a full, active life rooted in positive values and thinking. However his character was formed, Jimmie Storm was an outstanding person with true compassion, unquestioned integrity, and an honest and honorable desire to contribute. He cared for people and believed in selfless giving and public service.

Jimmie was an original builder of history's first mobile rig capable of operating in at least 100 feet of water. As a world-recognized pioneer in offshore drilling, he could have lived almost anywhere. Corpus Christi was fortunate that he chose it as home. His capabilities and generosities touched many aspects of this community as he truly enhanced the quality of life in this part of the country.

The recipient of his most distinguished public service was the Port of Corpus Christi Authority, which he served from 1973 until his death last month. He was first appointed a commissioner and then elected chairman in 1983. Port commissioners are appointed by the Nueces County Commissioners Court and by the Corpus Christi City Council, and are, accordingly, accountable to those bodies.

Jimmie helped guide the Port of Corpus Christi to become the nation's sixth largest port. His effective leadership, fiscal conservatism, and astute judgment were instrumental in helping the port realize its current strong financial and competitive position. A respectable cash reserve exists after major capital investments and improvements. The port is a unique public asset. Its strength is essential to the long-run health of the economy of this region.

During the last year of his life, Jimmie expressed his concern to certain family members and close friends about what could happen to the port when he was gone. In his gentle and quiet manner, he described the port as a microcosm of issues facing the country; he communicated his strong views of how the public's business should be conducted. One of his unfinished goals was to develop and implement a code of ethics for the port and its commissioners. As port chairman, he did all within his power to conduct the port's business without political considerations, and free of conflicts of interest, or even the appearance of such. The integrity of people and project was very important to him.

Port commissioners, led by their chairman, make decisions that govern millions of dollars and affect thousands of people. Complex and difficult issues require knowledge, judgment, and objective non-self-interested decision-making to properly serve the public interest and maintain its confidence.

Jimmie Storm's legacies to the Port of Corpus Christi include its condition and the standards that he envisioned being upheld and sustained in terms of the integrity of the authority, its commissioners, and their decision-making and conduct. Some work, vigilance, and follow-through may be necessary to ensure the continuity of these legacies.

As citizens, we have the power to oversee the appointment and re-appointment process to the Port Authority by the county commissioners and City Council when we vote to elect, or re-elect, those who make the appointments. We can watch more closely their choices and their actions.

It will be easier for us to carry out our public responsibility while remembering Jimmie Storm than it will be to find among us many people who genuinely care as much for their fellow citizens and their community as did he.

In his words, "Nothing else in life is really lasting except what you do for others. The rest just doesn't matter very much."

Jack Ryan Will Be Remembered By All Who Knew Him

(Published August 15, 1992)

For almost half a century, life in this part of the country was enhanced by the presence among us of a person with special personal gifts. He had a world-class personality. He was exceptionally "cheerful, charitable, competent," with an exuberant, friendly manner that had no equal. He cared about people and had a way of communicating that to those whom he knew and met; his infectious smile assured that he never met a stranger. He was continuously asking people how they were doing, how were their family members, and concluded almost always with a, "Good to see you."

Jack Ryan was someone who made me feel truly welcome and at home in South Texas when I moved here in the latter 1970's. His and my wife's families had been friends for a long while. One of my first business dealings in this area was with Jack, who had integrity, and did exactly what he said he would do. His sudden death a few weeks ago has left all those whose lives he touched with a sense of genuine loss.

Jackson S. Ryan was an original. "They threw away the mold after Jack," one friend would remark. "If Jack hadn't been born, someone would have had to invent him," said another. He loved people and he loved living life to the fullest. He seemed forever positive and youthful in attitude, irrespective of the passage of time.

His interest in, and accomplishments related to, young people are among Jack's many legacies. He was a distinguished member and president of the Corpus Christi Independent School District Board of Trustees and a devoted alumnus and former trustee of Southern Methodist University. He was a former trustee of Corpus Christi State University.

Jack was a committed civic and community leader who contributed in many ways to South Texas. He was a real estate developer, entrepreneur, banker, rancher, and philanthropist. While his specific accomplishments are noteworthy, Jack Ryan will be remembered best for his unique personal attitude, manner, and style. He was one of a vanishing breed of Texas cattlemen, and of person, who truly enjoyed life and shared his warm, passionate, positive approach to living with those who knew him. Jack was among the best and last of those strong, natural, rugged individuals who marked an earlier era in Texas.

In difficult, challenging, and changing times, Jack will be especially missed for his cheerful, open disposition and relaxed way of handling stress. No matter how unhappy or down he would be, he projected a positive personality. He accepted adversity and success with equanimity. In Kipling's words, he "met with triumph and disaster, and treated those two imposters just the same." He had solid, basic values and was not confused about what mattered and what was most important to him.

People were important to Jack; whether someone was more or less successful was not relevant. Jack treated people from all walks and stations in life with equal respect and warm friendliness. He knew so many people in so many places. At monthly board meetings where I sat next to Jack for several years, he seemed to have more insights into more people than almost all of the other board members combined.

Jack had great character - and was one. Like most of us, he was not a saint - nor did he ever pretend to be. He was what he was - and conveyed it honestly. He was a dynamic, enthusiastic individual who knew how to have fun without hurting others. He seemed to experience life as an art form that is being lost in our increasingly complex, burdened society. Some of his actions and exploits were legendary. He could tell stories, with or without an occasional embellishment, like no one else; he appreciated the humor of life. We shall be telling "Jack Ryan stories" for years to come with fondness and love.

Jack Ryan will long be remembered by his family and legion of friends for his appreciation of beauty and life. Jack, it was always, "Good to see you," and wonderful to have been with you.

State Help Is Needed For M.D. Anderson

(Published December 10, 1994)

Virtually all Texans who have had cancer affect their lives, or the lives of their families or friends, are familiar with the University of Texas M. D. Anderson Cancer Center in Houston. It has been a world-recognized leader in research and treatment of cancer for over half a century. Its existence is a source of pride and hope for many people.

The next session of the Texas Legislature, opening next month, may well determine the future of M.D. Anderson. It is at a critical crossroad.

M.D. Anderson faces four serious challenges. First, the health-care marketplace, led by managed care and industry consolidation, has led to dramatic change and requires adaptation for survival. Secondly, the state's support for M.D. Anderson's operating budget has dropped in half in percentage terms since 1985. Third, state law requires M.D. Anderson to provide unlimited charity care for Texas residents without the ability to bill counties for indigent patient care services. These costs have soared from $35 million in 1985 to $199 million currently. Finally, state law requires physician referral for patients to go to M.D. Anderson; no other hospital in Texas has such a restriction.

Managed care administrators are increasingly making decisions formerly made by physicians, which is reducing patient access to M.D. Anderson.

The solutions to these threats to M.D. Anderson's future require internal initiatives, which are being taken, and action by the Legislature and the governor. The statutory changes needed include those to provide specific amounts of state appropriations to be designated for uncompensated charity care as well as for research and education. A formula-driven allocation of the general revenues to the counties needs to be developed for indigent patient care.

All Texans deserve access to the cutting edge cancer care and clinical research available at M.D. Anderson. Multidisciplinary services provided by M.D. Anderson offer the best hope for long-term survival and cure. The majority of the more than 315,000 patients registered since 1944 have been Texans. Over 26,000 residents of the 48-county South Texas region have been patients at M.D. Anderson over the past 50 years. During 1993, M.D. Anderson cared for 12 to 13 percent of all new cancer patients in Texas; 956 of those new patients were from South Texas.

Many people might not be alive without advanced therapy available at M.D. Anderson. One young, energetic second-grader today is 8-year old Christen Coronado. At age 4, she was diagnosed with a rare type of malignant brain tumor. Her parents, who then lived in Sinton, were terrified. After a golf ball-sized tumor was removed by surgeons in Corpus Christi, Christen was referred to M.D. Anderson for therapy pioneered there. It worked.

Courageous and decisive action must be taken in coming months to assure that our children and grandchildren can be treated successfully either for rare brain tumors like Christen had - or any of the other 100-plus types of cancer. We are fortunate to have outstanding medical care available in this area; an important complement is the accessibility of the vital resources of M.D. Anderson for those who need them. The wisdom and action shown by the generation of Texans who established M.D. Anderson must now be succeeded by our commitment to that which is necessary to preserve M.D. Anderson for today's and future generations.

Ride With Officers Gives A Close Look At Crime

(Published March 18, 1995)

"Few of us realize how close we are to the edge of violence," a friend said recently after participating in the Corpus Christi Police Department's "Ride-Along" program.

I have been a "citizen observer" and highly recommend this experience to anyone who wants to be a more informed citizen about our police department and how it deals with crime in our city.

One has the opportunity to ride with an officer on patrol, see what he does, and witness activities which are not part of most people's typical days and nights.

The Uniform Crime Report offers statistics that confirm the effectiveness of our police department.

Last year, homicides reported here were the lowest since 1963; the burglary rate was the lowest in 20 years. For the last full year when state and national figures were available (1993), the rate for solved homicides in Corpus Christi was 91 percent compared to a national rate of 65 percent, a Texas rate of 69 percent, and a rate for cities of our size of 62.5 percent.

While the statistics are positive, real validation comes from seeing the police department in action while riding with an officer. The communications, procedures, dedication, and coordination that I observed are exemplary.

What is especially noteworthy is the conduct of the officers in a variety of different situations, ranging from routine to false alarms to dangerous.

Significant credit for the capability of the department is due its leadership, especially Chief Henry Garrett. He is very committed to his work. His home phone number is listed, which is rare for someone in his position. It is consistent with his and the department's "How can I help you?" attitude.

Each "Ride-Along" participant will have his or her most memorable impressions, depending upon events. Nonetheless, certain common observations prevail among those who have ridden along.

One is that alcohol or drug abuse is the most frequent cause of problems. Another is the question of why the criminal court justice system doesn't perform more satisfactorily. Repeat offenders seem to generate a disproportionate share of police work. Serious offenders are often back on the street too early.

Community involvement and the attitudes of citizens in cooperation with the police department are crucial for success in maintaining a safe city; both are present here.

Our Neighbors on Watch and Crimestoppers programs are examples of an active citizenry. We can take pride in Corpus Christi as one of the nation's least likely places for people to watch a serious crime being committed and do nothing. This has not been the case in other cities - to their shame.

Finally, family issues are rarely more poignant or painful than when they become the subject of a call to the police. The plight and sorrow of adults and children in truly troubled families are very moving. The officers try to connect the families with appropriate help whenever possible.

Ride-along participants usually return to their lives with a different perspective after witnessing some of what occurs around this town. They have a greater appreciation of the challenges and contributions of police work. Everyone is encouraged to sign up -- at least once.

City Takes Major Stride Forward

(Published January 11, 1997)

CPP shows how communities can take the initiative.

Recent elections have made clear that the majority of the American public want a smaller federal government that is not deficit-financed, especially for ineffective social and economic programs. Many of our needs in those areas may be addressed best on a state, community, and private basis; volunteering and the standards of citizenship which have traditionally made our country great are being encouraged.

In such changing times, a priority is to identify ways for people, families, neighborhoods, communities, and others concerned about social problems and how to expand economic vitality to take positive action.

The proposals of Corpus Christi's Community Progress Partnership (CPP) represent such action and place this city in the forefront of important national priorities. For its thoughtful recommendations, including innovative thinking about trust funds, the CPP merits our support. CPP Chairman Al Jones summarizes its recommendations as "a package of programs and projects that would make a significant difference to our community's quality of life and economic vitality while addressing social and youth problems."

This joint effort of volunteers from all parts of the city, the Alliance, and the City Council is a great credit to Corpus Christi and "our bridge to the next century." The CPP connected all parts of our community into a cohesive unit. A comprehensive package of improvements has been proposed to develop projects targeted for our young people, specific City Council district needs, and public safety. The projects are to be funded by a combination of half-cent sales tax applied for 15 years plus state and federal matching grants.

Public forums will be held to offer more ideas for discussion to consider suggested refinements and to confirm that there are no significant omissions or duplications. The CPP final proposal will go to the City Council, which would schedule its submission to the voters.

Questions have an important role in our democracy and must be considered, but this is a great opportunity for civic renaissance. When the final CPP proposals are submitted to the electorate, their implementation would be as described and implemented by City Council appointees subject to the standards of the rules of conduct spelled out in the City Code of Ethics. The CPP proposals reflect no vested interest, or personal advantage. They are truly community-minded and reflect the high standards of public-spiritedness that have shaped America.

A community's strength is its ability to change, to revitalize, and to drive toward a promising tomorrow, not be left behind. The components of the CPP proposal make a positive contribution to our community and to enriching the lives of our citizens. It is effective allocation and management of our resources, including those coming from non-residents and matching grants.

Those responsible for the CPP understood our city's needs and have responded in an exemplary manner to them, which also is consistent with emerging national realities and responsibilities. The greatest country in the history of the world and each of its communities depend upon public-spirited citizens for their well being and strength. Each generation has had its challenges and requirements of individual responsibility collectively fulfilled. Ours is to re-affirm and re-dedicate to those civic and community values and standards, which led us to live here in the first place.

Section II

United States Economic and Business Issues

Curing Economy Takes Courage

(Published December 27, 1980)

Few experiences provide perspective like participation in the traditions that abound during the holiday season at year-end. It is a time for family and friends, for beautiful moments and cherished memories, for appreciation of living in this great country, and for considering the challenges and opportunities of the coming new year.

At this time of year in 1940, the prime rate in the United States was 1-1/2 percent and the nation was soon to demonstrate its courage and capability in the Second World War. Just before New Year's Day in 1960, the prime rate in this country was 4-1/2 percent and we were about to enter a period of significant change of values aimed at individual expression. On this Dec. 27, 1980, the prime rate is over 20 percent, and in my view, the country faces conditions that will require a combination of the courage and productive creativity of the past two generations.

The courage to which I refer is the resolve to wage a successful battle against the scourge of inflation. We cannot accept inflation at high levels as a fact of life; more than a short, painless effort is needed. Without major reduction, it will restrict economic freedom which will impact our political and intellectual freedom. Inflation is the most regressive, immoral tax - it falls hardest upon those who can least afford its consequences. A first class postage stamp that costs 15 cents would cost 27 cents in 1990 if inflation averages 6 percent until then or 50 cents if inflation averages 13 percent.

A number of actions and changes of direction are expected by the federal government to manage and then reduce almost $1 trillion of national debt plus other liabilities and guarantees that exist. As citizens, we can discourage continuous borrowing as a national habit: attitudes need to change and be communicated accordingly. Obligations should be satisfied by payment and not by serial extension of indebtedness to future generations. Our values should reward effort, saving, and capital formation. We should focus on the production of goods and services; too much attention has been paid by disparate interest groups to the distribution of capital. We need to create and produce more. This can take many forms if emphasis is placed on creation and productivity to enrich our lives and spirit and not programs to encourage inactivity. The world is increasingly too competitive to be complacent. Effort and work are left to the highly motivated while others, due to certain socially concerned but poorly conceived rules, have little incentive.

The beginnings of the scores of years in the latter part of the twentieth century have provided great challenges to the generations of Americans who responded to the main currents of the times in which they lived. Their actions affected their own lives and those who followed them. In the '40s, the defense of freedom was paramount: in the '60s, the extension of the benefits of freedom was pursued. In the '80s also, courage and productive creativity are going to be required to preserve a way of life based upon individual freedom.

Reagan's Goals Worth Risk

(Published February 28, 1981)

"What is radical in this country today is not this administration's economic policy, but, rather the conditions that we face. Not since World War I has the United States experienced double-digit inflation in two consecutive years as it did in 1979-80." So began Budget Director David Stockman's comments at a meeting that I recently attended in Washington. He continued, "We are determined to address the underlying causes of these conditions."

During conversations with some of the thought leaders responsible for the administration's economic program - Mssrs. Stockman, Kemp, Wanniski and Ture - one had to be impressed with their commitment to fundamental change from the past and their willingness to take calculated risks to return the nation to the tax rates and money growth under which we previously prospered. The elements of President Reagan's economic program - spending cuts, tax reduction, deregulation, and a consistent monetary policy - are expected to reinforce each other in altering our complex, modern economy.

Three observations about the president's economic program seem appropriate:

• Most importantly, the president is building confidence that he will do what he says he will do. In his Inaugural Address, he articulated his first priority of renewing economic strength; his comprehensive, innovative, long-range program offers a realistic opportunity to do just that. The priority of, and focus upon, his economic agenda reinforces its credibility; people are believing and they want to believe. The program, while not ideal, and not without short-term dislocations for everyone, is an excellent beginning. While a number of specifics may be changed in the legislative process, the broad outlines of the president's economics are responsive and responsible and should be sufficient to provide necessary re-direction away from accelerating inflation.

• The program's actual impact on inflation and stimulation of real growth and productivity will take time; in this age of instant gratification, the president has taken the initiative to begin to turn the current inflation psychology; he will need sustained support from the public for the effort to be successful. There will be many criticisms, controversies, and challenges before implementation.

• The president has recommended a plan directed toward changing the course of U.S. history as significantly as it was changed earlier in this century with Roosevelt's New Deal. The boldest single part of the program challenges previously accepted economic theory and places limits on expectations about the role of the federal government. This administration is committed to translating supply-side economics into policy. The policy seeks to restore incentive and reduce entitlements except for the truly needy. It advances a philosophy of major tax reduction to encourage the private sector to develop within its own dynamics. It seeks to increase production and economic growth by encouraging savings, capital formation, and investment; this should help restore stable, long-term capital markets.

The president's words and actions provide a basis for confidence. He envisions a truly strong economy, and therefore, country, emerging once again. The promise of his plan is clearly worth the risk.

President Ronald Reagan
AP/WIDE WORLD PHOTOS.

Flat Rate Tax Cure For Woes

(Published May 15, 1982)

One idea to strengthen our economy is a bold innovation, i.e., a complete change in approach to federal income taxation. The federal income tax was a simple, almost flat rate program when first enacted in 1913. Today, the tax code is a nightmare of confusing and complicated regulations which are constantly being altered or re-interpreted.

A comprehensive tax system with either moderately progressive rates or a flat rate should be adopted. All income - from individuals and corporations - would be taxed. The new approach would eliminate all deductions, special credits, loopholes, bracket creep, marriage penalties, success penalties, etc. Recently, this idea has been discussed by thoughtful leaders across the political spectrum. One U.S. senator has introduced legislation entitled a "Flat Rate Tax Act of 1982."

A comprehensive tax system would be easy to understand and administer - and would be fair. Over a certain minimum, all income would be taxed at the same rate. The minimum would be set at a level, which would provide adequate protection for lower income families. If all income beyond a certain minimum were taxed, for example, at 16 percent, many important advantages could be achieved.

Knowledgeable economists advise that such an income tax would easily balance the 1983 federal budget. Interest rates would be reduced and the economy stimulated properly. According to the Congressional Budget Office, the revenue loss from tax loopholes under the present system is estimated to be in excess of $250 billion for the current fiscal year. Under this comprehensive approach, the tax base would be increased and the national interest served.

Further, more resources would be allocated according to basic supply and demand factors rather than to tax considerations. Long-term investment commitments could be made without concern that the next Congress will again change tax guidelines. This would be of great value to our domestic economy and to our international competitive position.

Also, the economic cost of complying with a federal income tax can be significantly reduced. For example, someone in another state that has a flat income tax recently completed his one-page return in ten minutes. His federal return required 38 pages and took more than six hours of expert preparation.

Adhering to our present code reinforces voter apathy both in the difficulty of understanding it and in its violation of a sense of fairness that everyone should contribute to the cost of government. With existing shelters and loopholes, little or no tax is paid on very significant amounts of income. The change recommended would make operative the principle that all who receive the benefits of living in this country should share in the cost of government. A flat tax would also minimize the feeling of being overwhelmed by unproductive bureaucracy represented by lengthy tax forms.

Moreover, the present system tends to undermine important personal standards; it does not encourage honesty. The underground economy with its "cash only" dealings and "barter exchanges" includes a huge number of unreported transactions.

Two other observations seem appropriate. One is that opposition to a comprehensive tax system may be expected primarily from those special interests which consistently beat the system and pay little or no tax in relation to income. Secondly, the current tax system provides indirect incentives through tax reduction to encourage certain activities, such as real estate development. These same objectives can be accomplished by direct incentives; clear priorities could be recognized as such rather than obscured deep in complex regulations.

Grace Commission Survey Offers Way Off The Treadmill

(Published May 27, 1984)

The President's Private Sector Survey on Cost Control (PPSS) was established in June of 1982 with J. Peter Grace as its chairman. Its mission was to identify inefficiencies, overlap, and waste in the federal government. The Grace Commission was the first complete review of the operations of the executive branch of the federal government since the second Hoover Commission during the 1950's. The survey was directed by business executives, plus representatives from labor and academia; both political parties and independents were represented on the executive committee of this privately funded, in-depth review.

After 18 months of analysis, the commission recommended 2,478 improvements in government operations, contained in 47 reports, 21,227 pages of material, and 1.5 million pages of supporting documentation, with estimated savings of $424.4 billion over three years. These savings can be achieved without raising taxes, without weakening America's defense build-up, and without harming necessary social welfare programs.

Program waste and inefficiency, systems failures, and personnel mismanagement account for 95 percent of $424.4 billion in estimated savings. On the basis of 1983 federal spending, PPSS recommendations would reduce defense expenditures by 11.7 percent, welfare spending by 7.1 percent and other government functions by 10.2 percent.

Federal mismanagement occurs at a time when we are facing deficits in the $170-$200 billion-plus range for the foreseeable future. If current spending and revenue patterns continue, in the year 2000 alone the deficit will be $2 trillion. Our currency is being debased daily and still government spending grows. In 1948, federal spending was 12 percent of GNP; in 1962, 20 percent; and in 1983, 25 percent.

There are three possible courses to take with regard to the uncontrolled growth in federal spending: (1) ignore the problem, (2) cover it up, or (3) fix it.

(1) We have been doing an excellent job of ignoring the problem for many years, mainly by using federal accounting systems which hide more than they show, are understood by very few, provide no control, and which would lead any normal entity into bankruptcy.

(2) Covering the problem is easy - focus on the deficit and "solve" the deficit by raising taxes. Since the median income family paid $2,218 in taxes in 1983 compared to $9 in 1948 - taxes up 32.4 times the increase in income over the period - how much more can we tax? Even if we were to confiscate the earnings of the "rich" (all untaxed income above $75,000), we would have enough to run the country for only 10 days.

(3) The only practical solution is to reduce federal spending and the sooner that is recognized the sooner fiscal sanity can be restored.

The Grace Commission report does not claim perfection, but it is an insightful, well-documented series of recommendations that can produce results - and soon, if implemented with a sense of urgency.

The survey needs public support since 73 percent of its recommendations require congressional approval. We need our democracy working for the American public, not for special interest groups. The Grace Commission report is not a complete answer to the problem; its adoption, nonetheless, is a necessary step in the only direction that we should choose to go.

The Nation's Focus in 1992 Will Be On The Vital 'E' Issues

(Published October 12, 1991)

Economics and ecology are two forces, which have clearly been driving much of the world recently. Economics prevailed over communism in the Soviet Union and Eastern Europe, loosened apartheid in South Africa, and was the underlying reason for the Gulf War. Ecology - including phenomena related to air, land, and water pollution, the ozone layer, and preservation of nature's wonders - is increasingly affecting people's behavior throughout the world. These forces are powerful in our country, and may be expected to be especially so as we enter the time of being within one year of a national election.

Moving toward November of 1992, the quadrennial season for debate and analysis of the issues of our time is beginning. Based upon experience, we may anticipate presidential and congressional campaigns to simplify ideas and issues into short commercials and catch phrases. Accordingly, we might prepare ourselves by thinking of the election of 1992 as "E-time," for most of the significant domestic issues can be described by words beginning with that letter.

They include education, employment, enforcement of our criminal laws, effectiveness of government, eradication of our drug sub-culture, and ending urban and family decline. Economics and ecology are at the core of national concerns about erosion in our quality of life.

The economic issues that we face are not the comprehensive problems confronting those countries now undergoing fundamental change to a market economy, but ours are serious and far-reaching, nonetheless. Many challenges exist for our economy, national debt position, and financial system. Our ecology issues are similar to those encountered around the globe, but are more extensive because our historical industrial success caused environmental damage largely ignored in prior eras.

As we move forward to address these economic and ecological issues, they will frequently be inter-related. Along with other nations, we need to balance pressures to create or maintain viable economies that will satisfy the needs of growing populations, and the real danger that uncontrolled growth will cause ecological disaster. An effective partnership among business, environmentalism, and government is required to not lose the planet by default either to poverty and war on the one hand, or to planet-wide disruptions in the process of nature on the other.

In short, we must recognize the legitimate needs and aspirations of a world at the end of the 20th century in balancing economic interests and environmental consciousness. Government's role is a vital one.

It is up to the government to lead - to point the way - to encourage, and, if necessary, to penalize more than it has to date. Recent developments are encouraging. The Justice Department issued new guidelines to encourage businesses to uncover environmental wrongdoing within their ranks and to address it with reduced exposure to potential serious liability. Required packaging disclosures are leading consumers to increasingly choose products for their ecological attributes as well as for price, design, label, or whatever. A third development was the introduction of the Gulf of Mexico Preservation Act of 1991, which is aimed at giving preservation of the Gulf comparable priority to that accorded other large bodies of water such as the Great Lakes.

As "E-time" unfolds, we shall think about, and be concerned about, the shape of tomorrow's world. While a number of considerations will be important, above all, we must remember that,"for all of our wondrous works and soaring dreams, we depend for our lives on six inches of soil and the fact that it rains now and then."

At Century's End, Our Economy Is Stronger Than Ever

(Published March 27, 1999)

Spring traditionally welcomes a time of growth and expansion. During this last spring season of the 1900's, it seems appropriate to reflect on what history will undoubtedly recognize as the most powerful period of growth and expansion in this century, if not any century: the growth and strength of the American economy and capital markets during the past two decades.

My personal perspective on this remarkable period dates back to the spring of 1982. At that time, the economy was weak and interest rates were in double digits; the Dow Jones Average, which had broken the 1,000 mark in the late 1960's, hovered around 800; 10,000 was not foreseeable this century. Large budget deficits and competition from Asia, especially Japan, were troublesome. All pointed to a gloomy future.

A small group of business people had a breakfast meeting at the Federal Reserve in Washington with its then chairman, Paul Volcker. He asked if anyone thought that interest rates would continue higher and inhibit economic recovery and growth.

When one person answered affirmatively, one could never forget the sight of this six foot-eight-inch chairman rising from his chair. Chairman Volcker said, "that attitude was what was temporarily wrong with America." What was right was the fundamental confidence, optimism, and ability of the American people to overcome obstacles and build a better and better future. He pledged that such a future would have much lower interest rates trending to low single digits.

Both our economy and capital markets have surged since 1982, some reverses notwithstanding. More than 35 million net new jobs have been created, many from entrepreneurial new businesses. The quality of life of large numbers of Americans has been significantly improved by the growing changing economy. Many trillions of dollars of new wealth have been created. Common stock values have increased tenfold or far better; almost half of all American adults participate today as shareholders.

Stock market prices, of course, reflect the collective actions of millions of individuals and institutions that buy and sell. Many theories and reasons are given by Wall Street professionals and others as to what has propelled, and continues to drive the stock market. Low inflation, capital gains tax cuts, earnings growth, evolving foreign markets, an effective fiscal policy which balanced the budget, and the growth of retirement plans and mutual funds are among the reasons discussed. Many people, of course, have technical or chart-driven explanations. There is no shortage of experts in a bull market.

For me, however, the most insightful explanation is two-fold: (1) low interest rates which evolved in no small part due to the efforts of Paul Volcker and his successor Alan Greenspan, and (2) widespread confidence in our free enterprise system and our country.

The release of creative energies, combined with scientific and technological progress, have transformed our economy and capital markets. The stock market reflects anticipation of what the future holds; an optimism has existed about how we live, transfer information, and accelerate the pace of change to advance our country and its citizens, and humankind.

Chairman Volcker's advice on that spring day 17 years ago is worth remembering - do not make a long-term bet against a resurgent, resourceful, focused, confident America.

Paul Volcker
AP/WIDE WORLD PHOTOS.

Section III

United States Domestic, Social, Cultural and Generational Issues

All-Out War On Crime Due

(Published May 2, 1981)

While the passage of a comprehensive national economic program is still several months away, it appears that the legislation will be consistent with the position recommended by the president. The importance placed upon economic matters is appropriate. Nonetheless, it is not too early to identify the next area of focus for our domestic policy agenda.

I would submit that our next priority should be concentration upon actions calculated to significantly reduce violent crimes.

Violent crime is a problem that elicits strong emotion, is the subject of continuing media reports, but has somehow not yet been addressed with cohesive measures that produce results. When Supreme Court Justice Rehnquist writes in an opinion issued earlier this week that the country is "rapidly approaching a state of savagery" in which we "cannot provide security to our people in the streets or in their homes," he articulates the urgency for all citizens to speak out and correct these conditions.

The Justice Department recently reported that one in three American households were victimized by at least one crime in 1980. People are fearful and are buying burglar alarms, heavy locks, and weapons at a rapid rate; the security business has become one of the leading growth industries in the country! The prevalence of this violence and fear of violence should not be permitted to reduce freedom in our lives.

For several years, the United States has been the most violent industrial democracy. Many experts are currently looking at this issue, including a Task Force on Violent Crime that was recently appointed by the attorney general of the United States; it is difficult to conceive of why a comprehensive anti-violent crime program cannot be created and implemented with a sense of urgency and innovation. A central obstacle facing other programs - the proliferation of antagonistic special interest groups - should not be relevant here. What special interest group exists to defend violent criminals that is more powerful than a tidal wave of public demand for action?

The points that are made when people talk about this problem - the long delays in the judicial process, lack of consistent sentencing, plea bargaining inequities, the need for more respect for law enforcement capabilities, the need to attract and retain capable prosecutors, stiff punishment consistent with the crime not being imposed, and many others - should be considered and Domestic Agenda Priority Number Two should be pursued. We need to protect individual rights but not to such an extreme that it prevents the vast majority from being secure. People are tired of the perpetrator of violent crimes being "punished" by a light sentence when a victim loses a limb or a life.

Public policy should be taking us in the direction of more effective, tougher response to this problem area. Our emphasis should be on translating our priorities into programs that will ensure the safety of our children in their yards and of our president in his own country.

Nation Recognizing Crisis

(Published March 6, 1982)

"When you get into a tight place, and everything goes against you, till it seems as though you could not hold on a minute longer, never give up then, for that is just the place and time that the tide will turn."
- Harriet Beecher Stowe

In the past, when we were threatened, Americans experienced one event that impressed our national consciousness and got the attention and commitment of the whole country. The sinking of the Lusitania, the stock market crash of 1929, and Pearl Harbor provided clear, dramatic signals that we faced a crisis; it was immediately recognized and a unified nation rallied.

Today, we face a crisis that is no less serious in its ultimate challenge to our way of life, but it came upon us undramatically. Since the late 1960's, we have experienced a number of setbacks which relate to the erosion of our position from former heights which were unchallenged in the world. From Vietnam to Watergate, followed by our hostages in Iran, to our current international disappointments and domestic problems, we have increasingly become vulnerable and concerned on many fronts. Troublesome inflation was perceived as transitory years ago; federal budget deficits were viewed as temporary. Double-digit interest rates were seen as unsustainable when experienced in 1974. High crime levels would not continue here, we thought, as we also hoped our allies would be supportive.

These individual developments, and others, when viewed cumulatively, are very significant. Our "crisis by erosion" has put this country "into a tight place."

No single, catastrophic event, has yet to mobilize our attention and our energies; nonetheless, our present circumstance requires a comparable response as that given by previous generations when they were tested by clear crisis. Citizen resolve and participation, willingness to sacrifice and cooperate, placing of national interest above special interest, and a bipartisan approach to problem-solving have worked well for this country throughout our history; seemingly insurmountable problems were recognized and successfully met by these attitudes and their resultant actions.

Recently, I have been encouraged by a broader recognition of the seriousness of the "crisis by erosion" and by the response. Some examples include: (1) Unions and companies are beginning to cooperate in unprecedented ways. In the automotive, airline, steel, and other industries, labor and management are working together to solve mutual problems. (2) FBI Director Webster, at a meeting that I recently attended, observed that increasing community involvement in Crime Stoppers is one of the most important developments in law enforcement history. (3) Regulatory agencies and some of the companies with which they have been litigating for years are resolving disputes and redefining their relationship in light of current economic realities.

Further, increasing bipartisan approaches to serious problems are developing - even in an election year. A bipartisan National Commission on Social Security is focusing on that important and difficult issue. Representatives of both political parties are working together in Congress to pass a constitutional amendment this year establishing a balanced federal budget as a future requirement. Many Democratic and Republican legislators are acting like United States congressmen and senators in seeking bipartisan approaches to pressing problems.

In the past, we have had one event to alert us to mobilize our energies; everyone understood what was required. Our current "crisis by erosion" happened gradually. We need to respond by expanding cooperation and voluntary actions on a multitude of levels throughout our society. It is consistent with the elements of our historical tradition that have worked whenever the vast majority of Americans became aware, and then dedicated. I have confidence that "the tide will turn."

Path To Consensus Needed

(Published May 21, 1983)

Memorial Day is nine days from today. As we remember and honor those who gave their lives so that we may live in freedom, we should affirm our responsibility to achieve positive results in resolving some of the problems that threaten our democratic way of life.

The pages of this newspaper inform us daily of decay in vital national institutions; examples include an overloaded criminal justice system and a public school system that fosters mediocrity and functional illiteracy. "If an unfriendly foreign power had attempted to impose on America the mediocre educational performance that exists today, we might well have viewed it as an act of war." This statement is from a well-publicized recent national study.

The country is not solving many of its problems because "a national anesthesia" is applied to broad, significant problems while hundreds of personal preferences and selfish, narrow interests receive implementation.

The well organized and often selfish obtain results. The unorganized majority gets rhetoric, frustration, and more news about the problem. In recent years, special interest groups have become so strong that they, in effect, veto action on broad, important issues. The power to change is concentrated upon narrow benefits for a limited constituency.

In my view, a major reason that vital national problems linger without significant resolution is the collapse of an American consensus; this is reinforced by apathy and distrust of institutions that are not working. Neither Congress nor the president lead very often in these changing times. They follow where a consensus position has been achieved.

We are not solving important problems like the education of our people because vehicles have not yet come into existence that require all of the powerful interest groups that bear on an issue to come together and take action. When such an instrument of change is created, we get some results. This is consistent with the American tradition of innovating and developing what is necessary to solve problems. As an example, we were all kept well informed about the potential insolvency of the Social Security program. Finally, a bipartisan Commission on Social Security, comprised of representatives of all of the major constituencies, was created with a time frame to reach a conclusion. The diverse interests defined the problem and arrived at a compromise solution that was not ideal, but it worked and specifically addressed the problem.

To strengthen our institutions and our society, we must start obtaining meaningful results in dealing with these important problem areas, not just communicating the problems. A new perspective should include obtaining a sense of common destiny; a consensus among those that can effect change when mobilized.

As we see the need and the opportunity to advance our national interest - in education, in our criminal justice system, in national security, in the environment, and other important areas - let us encourage the creation of "vehicles of consensus" that result in action. It may not be all that some of us want, but it is a lot more than we have been getting, or will obtain if we do not reappraise and transform our national ability to get something done.

Community Cooperation Pays Off

(Published October 29, 1983)

When a community attracts a major new business, with its investment and employment, it is a noteworthy accomplishment. Fifty-eight cities in 27 states actively competed earlier this year to be selected as headquarters for such a venture. Austin was chosen and is now expected to be a focal point for a fast-growing industry; it is expected to draw related businesses and stimulate an entrepreneurial culture. It was, therefore, with great interest that I attended a meeting a few weeks ago to obtain some insight as to how Austin achieved this significant success.

The meeting was with Ret. Adm. Bobby Inman and some of the people who brought him and his company to Austin. Inman now heads a company called Microelectronics and Computer Technology Corporation (MCC). MCC is a consortium of high technology-oriented companies that agreed to fund a large research and development budget. The research will initially focus upon developing the first "fifth generation" computer system - a system with the ability to "think."

Many factors influenced MMC's location decision. They included outstanding organization and leadership by a public/private/academic team that represented many ideological views. When MCC reduced its choices to four cities in as many states, an effort led by the governor, which included San Antonio's mayor and businessmen from several cities, was effective.

When Dallas and San Antonio were eliminated, some of their leaders actively helped Austin. The University of Texas at Austin and Texas A & M University made significant financial and other commitments. "Those universities working together made a real impression," said Inman. The creation of a comprehensive "Texas Incentive for Austin" made a difference. The business climate, state and local dedication to supporting and improving primary and secondary education, and the overall quality of life were very important. Coordinated public and private commitments to fund a package of economic benefits to MCC made a critical difference.

MCC's location search had a specific requirement that a city have a major university with research capability in its field; this precluded consideration of Corpus Christi. Our higher education institutions can compete in situations which require an applied computer science capability. Nevertheless, Inman's observations are informative and instructive regarding how the goal of positive business development can be realized by a committed community in the mid-1980's.

Inman advised that an important factor is the prevailing attitude in a community that is under consideration. Most companies tend to be interested in those places in which people "constructively participate, not criticize and anticipate."

When an opportunity is identified and focused upon, only the cooperation of everyone working together will give a community a real chance for success in the serious competition to locate an attractive enterprise. State or other assistance may need to be mobilized to supplement a community's efforts and resources.

A community needs to be alerted early to new ventures and location searches that are announced on the national scene. A real contribution was made by the Austin citizen, who happens to be a city employee, who first read about MCC's formation in a technical journal. He informed the Chamber of Commerce and others interested in business development about the opportunity. The identification of potential opportunities for a city can and should involve the whole community.

If Only Life Was Like The Movies...

(Published July 14, 1984)

If you have had a love affair with movies for as long as you can remember, or if you know someone with this incurable condition, you know how especially lucky such people are this summer. They have a range of choices to provide absorbing entertainment away from the heat and drought for a few hours.

Movies like "The Karate Kid" and "The Natural" are positive, uplifting, and inspiring. Basic American values are communicated and reinforced. Pain, poverty, and other problems challenge the central characters. Those who work to develop themselves, acquire capability and confidence, and persevere are the ones who triumph over adversity. The concluding moments of these films are memorable.

All movies are not worth seeing. If you are suitably selective, however, you may receive much more satisfaction from good feature films than from observing other phenomena this summer. A list of unattractive sights includes candidates for responsible public office advocating positions which weaken our national defense and other highly questionable and naïve courses of action. It includes Soviet spokesmen feigning concern about the U.S. government as a reason not to attend the Olympics in two weeks. Perhaps if our government terrorized its citizens and chained those who seek freedom, the Soviets would feel more at home.

Other happenings that most of us do not support include a candidate for a major party's nomination for president severely criticizing this country and its foreign policy while praising totalitarian regimes in the presence of the leaders of those subjugated lands. Should anyone be confused by the propaganda of humanitarianism related to the trip in question, consider the words of Andre Vargas Gomez, imprisoned for 21 years by Castro, who was among those freed during candidate Jesse Jackson's trip: "To go to Cuba to join in a moral offensive with Fidel Castro is more than morally offensive; it is a moral offense." He added that there is "no negotiating with Castro or any Communist. It is an illusion and the people of the world should not be fooled."

One of the more regrettable byproducts of the intense competition for front-page and prime time coverage is what is done by some candidates to get attention. One would rather watch a good adventure or romantic movie than political opportunism in the guise of a real life success story.

The ironic fact is that a number of movies are excellent in terms of articulating fundamental American values while some aspiring office-holders are providing more negative performances than the great leadership which our country deserves.

The political conventions this summer and the fall campaign will better serve our citizens if the politicians concentrate on issues and leave entertaining and theatrics to Robert Redford, Michael Jackson, and to "The Return of E.T."

E.T.
AP/WIDE WORLD PHOTOS.

Arafat, Cowboys, And Kremlin Look For Winning Strategy

(Published January 7, 1989)

President-elect Bush called for a "kinder, gentler nation." One way of responding would be to address some of our serious issues with humor; such treatment may actually signal the beginning of a true turn in fortune.

For example, our state's currently most publicized financial institution, M Corp., recently ran a full page ad aimed at the Dallas Cowboys saying "1988 wasn't our year either." As we enter a new year, and perhaps, new era, it may be interesting to look into a 1989 crystal ball and attempt to apply a lighter perspective.

As last year, this will be a year of startling surprises; in fact, the trend may even accelerate.

Within weeks, Mikhail Gorbachev will invite two high-profile Americans to be guest speakers at the Kremlin. Tom Landry will talk about offensive and defensive strategies. "Assuming that they listen to his advice, which is what guided his team's performance last year," CIA Director Webster will report, "America has not been more secure in several generations."

Jesse Jackson will follow Landry and speak to the remaining hard-liners in the KGB and Red Army about glasnost. After hours of his rhetoric, the audience will clasp their ears and flee, seeking asylum anywhere they will not have to listen anymore.

Yasser Arafat will move to Paris to become a fashion consultant. His first client will be Fidel Castro who desperately wants to change his image.

Meanwhile, in our nation's capital, Vice President Quayle will get off to a bad start by being an hour late to the Inauguration because he had a late tee-off time and was caught in a traffic jam of people concluding their prayers for Bush's good health. Nonetheless, his image will improve during 1989 as he assembles a first-rate staff including Chi-Chi Rodriguez.

President Bush will select singer-musician Ray Charles to be his official lip-reader and interpreter of what he really means. The president will resist raising taxes; he will try to work with Congress, and will then turn to innovative approaches. Federal property will be sold. One former national treasure will become Trump Monument and the famous white building at 1600 Pennsylvania Avenue will become Honda House.

Michael Dukakis will visit Washington to give a lecture to the National Press Club reiterating that the issue of last year's election was competence; it was. Gary Hart will return to address the graduating class of CIA agents on the importance of exercising good judgment and being discreet.

Oliver North will revise President Kennedy's immortal words and say, "Ask not what you can do for your country because you may find out, do it, and then devote your life to defending what you did."

The federal government, having given us a staggering national debt and trade imbalance, will launch an investigation into the present non-problem of leveraged buyouts. Stung by this attack, a consortium of investment partnerships will immediately announce a takeover of the U.S. Treasury. However, after doing due diligence, they will conclude that too many actual and contingent liabilities exist and will withdraw their offer. Almost anything can be LBOed or refinanced - except the federal government, unless its budgeting process and institutional paralysis are corrected.

Two famous citizens will leave Washington. Ronald Reagan will move to California, and then will try to attend a 55th reunion celebration of Notre Dame, only to be informed by officials (again) that he really didn't attend college and play football there. Ted Kennedy will successfully return to Harvard as professor of Spanish and assistant swimming coach.

A number of significant issues will be addressed during 1989. In education, the three "r's" will officially be joined by a V - video. Regarding the related issues of an official language and literacy, English will remain our required language; however, when correct grammar and multi-syllable words are used, it will not be understood by most of our citizens. In the War on Drugs, a rumor will circulate that cocaine and crack induce hard work and the recognition of reality. Demand will decline.

Regarding individual values, that which is traditional and predictable will be appreciated far more and experienced far less. The exception to that will be all things Texan; the state's status and influence in the country and world will surge as prominent Texans express preferences for Lone Star favorites from country music to boots. True romance will continue to flourish, although Don Johnson and Melanie Griffith will rival Mike Tyson and Robin Givens as model couples.

In the world of finance, there will be some surprises and some non-surprises. The surprises will include interest rates, the price of oil and gold, and the direction of the stock market. The non-surprises will include Drexel, Burnham's payment of its $650 million fine out of part of its first quarter's profits and the Coastal Bend's continuing economic recovery.

Finally, 1989 will be a year of continuous change and challenge in international relations. Henry Kissinger will visit Corpus Christi in early March to interpret what is happening for us. He will emphasize the trend of Far Eastern capital and culture influencing our way of life. We shall be especially affected in South Texas when our best-known and liked food service company introduces the Whattawonton this spring.

If these prospects for 1989 concern you, try to relax and enjoy the year anyway. In only 51 weeks the decade of the 90's will begin and this year will be remembered as the good old days - a time when we were kinder and gentler.

President John F. Kennedy
AP/WIDE WORLD PHOTOS.

Last Decade Of The Century Holds Promise Of Great Change

(Published November 11, 1989)

Within weeks, we shall begin the last decade before entering the 21st century. The 1990s look to be a vibrant time and an appropriate way to end what will surely be remembered by our great-grandchildren as the American century. Our many problems and challenges notwithstanding, what has been achieved by our free United States of America has not been equaled by any other country in the history of the world.

The '90s promise to be exciting for many reasons; some merit comment today. At the essence of each is human nature, or the nature of cycles and rhythms, or the combination of both. The Chinese articulated the point in their ancient proverb, "The mandate of heaven is not forever." Evolution and change are to be planned for and expected.

Those eager for positive changes that produce results, vis-à-vis our national problems, should consider an interesting perspective. Historians refer to 30 years as the time frame of a generation. People tend to form their values, political views, and expectations between their mid-teens and mid-20s by the ideals prevalent at that time. When their generation assumes power approximately 30 years later, they renew and reinforce the inclinations of their youth. For example, Presidents Kennedy and Johnson grew up during a time of fundamental strategic change in the country spawned by the New Deal in the '30s. Their New Frontier and Great Society seized historic opportunities to effect change inspired in their youth, adjusted to the changing times and circumstances of the '60s.

Accordingly, as the rhythm continues, the generation formed during the '60s can be expected to translate the energy, the rebelliousness, and the reform-consciousness of that time into an agenda for the '90s. As cycles tend to adjust to recent excesses, their program should implement a number of changes that address our serious problems. Citizens will become more active and involved as apathy and alienation are replaced by involvement and action. If the pattern of the century continues, some effective leaders will emerge.

Further, there will be a convergence of reform as we grow stronger in the '90s, reinforcing the fact that democracy and freedom do work, with the worldwide move away from communism. The world's first communist state, the Soviet Union, has acknowledged the failure of communism both as a political structure and as an economic model. Communism doesn't work and has failed the tests of time, reality, and human nature. The immense challenges of converting communist nations to countries with their own forms of democratic principles and institutions will continue as we move toward the year 2000. As democratization evolves, the benefits of free exercise of expression, individual capability, and creativity will replace the burdens of terror and totalitarianism.

Ongoing crises are to be anticipated, but few now doubt that the Soviet Union and Eastern Europe are undergoing fundamental, strategic changes affecting virtually all aspects of their societies. The implications of the Gorbachev revolution are too extensive to discuss here beyond recognizing that the end of the '80s has ushered in a sea change of potential to transform the world.

A final observation about the interrelationship of human nature, cycles and the next decade is of special interest to us locally and throughout Texas. The 1990s will finally bring the long-awaited resurgence of the energy and related businesses. Industries, like people and nations, have their cycles and rhythms. The upswing of the cycle awaited by many and currently predicted by energy industry experts, some of whom live here among us, should be of significant benefit to our community.

Appeal Of Conscience League Promotes Religious Freedom

(Published November 17, 1990)

"We will bury you," then-Soviet Premier Krushchev warned the United States more than a generation ago in the midst of the Cold War. His threats were also directed toward ending all religious life in the Soviet territories by 1980. Accordingly, in 1965, an interfaith group of religious and secular leaders went to Moscow to begin a struggle to reverse the policy to eliminate all religions in the Soviet Union and Eastern Europe.

This unique ecumenical coalition of business and religious leaders returned from the Soviet Union and created the Appeal of Conscience Foundation. It is one of a number of relatively unknown and unheralded groups that merits far broader recognition. Its objectives are to preserve the rights of all religious groups throughout the world and to advance respect for human rights and individual dignity. The foundation celebrated its 25th anniversary a few weeks ago with its annual award dinner in New York. All living former presidents and secretaries of state of the United States were among those world leaders of business, religious and political life who support the Appeal of Conscience Foundation

This year's honorees were His Eminence Cardinal Agostino Casaroli, secretary of state of the Holy Sea and Jay A. Pritzker, prominent attorney and international businessman.

The timing of Cardinal Casaroli's recognition was coincident with the emerging realization of religious freedom and human rights in the Soviet Union and Eastern Europe. U.S. Ambassador to the United Nations Thomas Pickering praised the cardinal as a "prominent spiritual and political leader on the world scene for decades" and as one "devoted to translating ideals into the realm of practice. The Cardinal brought hope into those places in the world which were darkest." Former Secretary of State Henry Kissinger paid tribute to Cardinal Casaroli's patience, perseverance, and tireless efforts to alter communism.

Dr. Kissinger further recognized Jay Pritzker as a man "whose humanitarian devotion I have admired for many decades." Pritzker created the Pritzker Architectural Prize, which is now the architectural equivalent of the Nobel Prize. Jay Pritzker was honored for using his "business acumen to further education, mutual understanding and international cooperation."

As the honorees were recognized, one learned more about the foundation's activities. In addition to the Appeal of Conscience's tireless work in the Soviet Union and Eastern Europe, it sponsored the first interfaith delegation to visit the People's Republic of China. Meetings were held with the president of Cuba to improve religious life on that island. It brought together leaders from the various warring factions in Northern Ireland to begin a communication to try to ease the conflict there. The plight of the persecuted people of Tibet was highlighted.

These relentless efforts have achieved some very positive results. They are rooted in the conviction that the future of the world will belong to those nations that develop, nurture, and strengthen their religions and cultures, and respect the diversity of each. Where religious faith, tolerance, and respect for basic human values do not flourish, tyranny likely will.

It is appropriate, as we are about to enter that time of year when tradition, memory - even if painful - and perspective on life are most important, that we consider the Appeal of Conscience Foundation as an inspiration for what good, dedicated people can accomplish.

The issues of the 1960s were addressed by that generation. The challenges of the 1990s must now be met by another generation - with the values of the Appeal of Conscience serving as exemplary and motivational.

Henry Kissinger
AP/WIDE WORLD PHOTOS.

Can U.S. Solve Domestic Problems As Well As It Fights War?

(Published February 2, 1991)

Whether our nation has the will and ability to effectively solve the problems on our domestic agenda has been the subject of public debate for some time. Although obscured by the Gulf War, a frustration exists, because the problems are well recognized, but unified action has not been forthcoming.

An important aspect of the war in the Persian Gulf was that a consensus was reached in our country sufficient for action. We mobilized resources to meet the problem. Dissent was expressed, and continues to be, but such can be the strength of a democracy that is nonetheless capable of taking effective action.

The five-vote margin in the U.S. Senate was reminiscent of at least two other votes earlier in our national history which suggest that the existence of opposing viewpoints need not reflect upon the ultimate merits of a decision. The renewal of the draft, which enabled us to respond rapidly when our country was drawn into World War II, passed by only one vote. Abe Lincoln's decision to resupply Fort Sumner was the only "aye" vote in the Cabinet.

That the president and the Congress were able to be decisive, after extensive debate and to proceed to implement that which was determined to be in our national interest is significant. It shows that we still are institutionally capable of meeting certain challenges, i.e., immediate, highly visible, threatening to a vital interest, and responsive to specific aggression which directly challenges world peace and the rule of law. While our highest priority is to win the war and bring our brave men and women home, it may not be too soon to think about other kinds of crises; they are longer-term, less immediate than war with its minute-to-minute life or death consequences, but may be at least as important as the Persian Gulf in their ultimate effect.

Crises related to our national indebtedness, mediocre educational performance, our deteriorating social fabric and values, and other problems can hurt people in a different way than can a Scud missile or terrorist attack; the hurt is nonetheless destructive. The inability of cities and states to provide necessary public services, our weakened savings and banking system, increasing crime, our eroding economic competitive position, and our growing number of homeless and disenfranchised people are threatening to our way of life. The nation is at risk as much, but in a different way, and over a longer time horizon, as we are in the Persian Gulf.

We achieved a consensus and acted with a national resolve to address a highly visible, direct crisis - the aggression of Saddam Hussein. We need to show that we are equally capable of addressing longer term and corrosive problems in addition to those which are immediate and brutally challenging.

The philosopher William James challenged us to find the moral equivalent of war in order to mobilize the nation to address its non-defense problems. While he hated war, he acknowledged that it was sometimes necessary, as no effective alternative existed. When required, it satisfied a basic longing of people to be committed in a common cause fulfilling their duty to their fellow citizens and their country. No higher statement of, nor sacrifice for, patriotism can be made.

For some time, our country has been in a relative decline for complex reasons; one is that few people really act out of a sense of common sacrifice with, and responsibility to, their fellow citizens - such as they do in combat. One essential problem has been that people don't feel responsible personally for what happens in the country or even in their own communities. People don't vote or participate as they see a political system that avoids addressing the real problems and is paralyzed and irrelevant. Opinion polls have replaced leadership. The common cause that is experienced when America is at war unites our nation. It calls forth our best, as we see each day in the Persian Gulf.

The challenge to the greatest democracy and most successful country in the history of the world is how to mobilize itself to deal with the erosion in our way of life in the Midwest, the Northeast, the Southwest, and elsewhere as we have to meet a problem in the Middle East. We then must stay the course until our objectives are met and our national interest is advanced.

Will This Be The Generation That Lost A Generation Of Children?

(Published February 19, 1994)

One child said, "Bullets were everywhere. My friend was shot 17 times and killed. This happened right near our school. I am scared all the time." A 14-year-old has lost five friends to gunfire since she was 12. Another cried as she expressed her wish to have one more conversation with her father who was killed during a mugging while walking near her school to meet her.

This is not the testimony of young people in Sarajevo, Sudan, or Somalia. Nor is it the product of the imagination of a Hollywood scriptwriter. These reports are from white, black and Hispanic children testifying before the U.S. House Judiciary Committee's Crime Subcommittee earlier this month.

These 11 children who testified were from chronically troubled and violent schools throughout the United States. While we are fortunate not to have the worst of these conditions in South Texas, we are not immune from the underlying social and economic problems which lead to these tragedies; they are found in virtually every community.

The story of these young people surrounded by violence was told, but soon superceded, by other national and international news. But it is too moving and troubling to be forgotten.

It's hard to accept that this nation has so lost its way as to have American children in war-zone equivalents within our borders. The sacrifices of too many of our fellow citizens on battlefields around the world were not made throughout our history to preserve these conditions.

We remember the United States as a world leader that exercised its will and used its capabilities to deal firmly with those who committed atrocities in foreign lands. Our economic, political, and military power produced stability and peace. We helped rebuild nations in Europe and in the Pacific and created a secure time and place with hope for the future.

Listening to those young people tell about their lives and circumstances in parts of today's America was a warning of how far we have regressed in such vital spheres as assuring the physical safety of our young people and caring about them. Now we must concentrate on rebuilding at home for we must recognize and accept that we are creating a lost generation of children.

The term "lost generation" was used earlier in the century to describe a group of intellectuals, including some of our greatest authors, artists, and musicians, such as Ernest Hemingway, Gertrude Stein, Josephine Baker and F. Scott Fitzgerald. These individuals were intelligent, well educated, often affluent, and able to devote time to seeking personal insight and fulfillment in foreign cultures between two violent wars. Their challenge was seeking personal understanding.

Ironically, the term "lost generation" can be applied today as we approach the end of the century to a vastly different group. The children of today's lost generation are under-educated, primarily poor, and struggling to survive in a violent environment. Their challenge is personal survival.

Members of today's lost generation have some ideas to recommend to alleviate these shocking conditions. While adults and policy-makers struggle to address the highly complex and troubling issues, these children testifying provided straightforward solutions; a balance of certain constructive and rehabilitative efforts combined with enforcing no-nonsense punishment. They all asked for more after-school programs like Boys and Girls Club and more parental involvement and attention from adults. They also recommended swift and certain punishment for youthful offenders irrespective of age "as long as they knew what they were doing."

In Texas, for example, a young violent offender can only be confined until age 21 unless certified and tried as an adult. Those youngsters who have experienced violence strongly recommend that youths who kill be imprisoned for life.

These children asked for help "to feel safe." The future of a society can be forecast by how it cares for its young. If we do not respond to the basic safety and security needs of America's children, history may condemn us as "the generation that lost a generation of children."

Ernest Hemingway
AP/WIDE WORLD PHOTOS.

F. Scott Fitzgerald
AP/WIDE WORLD PHOTOS.

Society's Worship Of Celebrities Overlooks Real Heroes

(Published May 14, 1994)

Who recognizes the name of Tonya Harding or Nancy Kerrigan? Who recognizes the name of Johann Olay Koss or Duncan Kennedy?

The response demonstrates a serious problem of our time, vis-à-vis, the blurring and the confusion between celebrities and genuine heroes, caused, in part, by excessive, continuing media coverage of the former.

In fairness to the media, demand usually influences the product that's supplied. As a society, we are fascinated by bizarre behavior, by conflict, and by an apparently insatiable interest in that which is negative or sensational.

The violent, the visible, and the vulgar receive attention more frequently than those who conduct themselves positively. A preoccupation with bad and shocking news has been harmful to our society; modern communications have greater impact and reach than those of earlier times.

Historically, we revered and celebrated worthy, great heroes. Their actions reinforced the most cherished values and beliefs in our culture, i.e., moral courage to correct injustice, battlefield bravery, or sacrifice in order to help others or to assist a worthy cause. Heroes behaved admirably in a situation or in a defining time in life. Efforts to instill values in young people that help form good character are reinforced by visible, positive role models.

True heroes, such as Johann Olay Koss and Duncan Kennedy, can forecast the future as symbols and examples for our youth, but today, few remember them. Hype or other phenomena have been obscuring the difference between celebrities and heroes, and reducing the length of time devoted to maintaining worthy people in the public's memory.

The public's apparent interest in celebrities is reinforced by the way they are embraced, accepted, and followed on an on-going basis irrespective of objective merit. Ironically, as our ability to communicate through advanced print and electronic media has increased, the content and character of our heroes has been diminished by being blurred with celebrities of lesser accomplishment.

We often confuse a celebrity with a hero, notoriety with character, fame with virtue, and fortune with merit. This leads to excessive attention being paid to the undeserving and insufficient recognition being given to the meritorious.

Neither our country nor this community is well served by not differentiating coverage between celebrity for tawdry or inconsequential reasons and heroism for noble and admirable conduct.

An example of the problem occurred before, during and after the Winter Olympics. The pathetic Tonya Harding-Nancy Kerrigan case was celebrated to such an extent that it became a central story, often taking precedence over the Olympics. Celebrity status was extended to both young women, who continued to receive subsequent coverage, inferring heroic dimensions.

Two of the genuine heroes of the Winter Olympics, speed-skater Johann Olay Koss of Norway and luge team member Duncan Kennedy of the United States were recognized, but not as prominently or continuously as they deserved.

Gold medal-winning Koss went to Eritrea in East Africa to be with children who were orphaned in a war to show them that "you are not alone in this world." He annually hosts an event for disabled youngsters; one of them, a blind boy, was his guest in the stands as Koss set a world record.

Duncan Kennedy didn't win a medal, but he was a real hero, nonetheless, as he endured a beating to protect one of his teammates from a likely worse fate.

Countless other examples may be found on an Olympian, international, national, or community level.

The potential long-term significance of positive news stories about genuine heroes, including outstanding volunteers who live among us, is great. When this newspaper focuses on positive role models, it is especially important to the youth of this area. Such attention recognizes outstanding citizen-volunteers and other people demonstrating truly heroic qualities in the way that they lead their daily lives.

The Jefferson Volunteer Award recipients' profiles last month were an important contribution to positive role model development. So also are the many other good news and success stories for which the *Caller-Times* was recently honored by the Texas Associated Press with its top 1993 award, Community Service.

Celebrity worship and hero recognition and adoration should not be confused. By so doing, we deprive ourselves and future generations of positive role models that reinforce those values that we want to emphasize and perpetuate as a society. The heroic should triumph over the violent and the vulgar not only in the movies, but also in far more of our news stories and our popular folklore. Accordingly, in the future, more people will recognize the names, and remember the conduct and character of people like Johann Olay Koss and Duncan Kennedy.

What's Right With America?

(Published July 1, 1995)

July 4, 2000 is five years away, the first Independence Day of a new century. During a recent trip abroad, where it is sometimes easier to see the United States more clearly than it is at home, I reflected on that future and the position our country might have in the world in the 21st century.

We tend to be self-critical and are very aware of what's wrong with America. Conventional wisdom has foretold that the American Century will end by 2000 and that the coming century will be most influenced by another country or countries because this country is in serious and irreversible decline. Paul Kennedy said as much in "The Rise and Fall of the Great Powers." Some troubling forecasts and current realities notwithstanding, significant factors account for our global leadership. Accordingly, it is appropriate to consider that the promise for the future of America is such that the 21st century may be viewed in retrospect as having been as much of an American century as the 20th.

For much of history, the people of the world experimented with dictatorships, monarchies, ideological governments, and others, but most of them now seek democratic forms of government. The American experience with democracy is the model for the world; our success with institutionalizing and perpetuating freedom while improving the standard of living for our citizens is unequaled.

The size and strength of our economy is formidable. Despite its inefficiencies and inequities, our market-driven economy has weathered many challenges; other state-run economies have failed. The United States now even appears capable of addressing its budget deficits and national debt issues. Our ability to change our government democratically over time can be frustrating and requires patience but it has been important to our success.

Our entrepreneurial leadership is unrivaled. Original thinkers, pioneers, and builders in many fields - including medicine, communications, health care, computers, science, and a number of high-tech industries - are based in this country. This is the world's premier center for creativity and innovation.

Our educational system continues to be an important contributor to our preeminence. This priority area needs more attention and resources, although we have achieved a measure of academic excellence, especially at the university level.

We have no major international economic competitors. Europe is not coming together. Russia is a second-tier country. Japan has major internal problems, with more, including in real estate and banking, to be faced. While Japan is the world's second wealthiest country, its culture resists change and its business/government interconnection may provide short-term advantages but, in the long term, will stifle creativity.

In an increasingly interdependent world, racial and religious tolerance combined with multiculturalism will be essential to domestic peace and progress. Sexual equality continues to emerge as similarly important. This country leads in all of these areas. Other countries may appear to profess more tolerance, but when tested - i.e., Britain, with its immigration issues - will often fail.

Our armed forces maintain a proud history of using power when necessary and not in occupying other nations. Our military capability provides a required underpinning to our security and way of life in a still turbulent and potentially more dangerous world.

With respect to the environment, the rest of the world will need to upgrade its standards and act more responsibly. The United States is further ahead in this vital area.

One hundred years ago, only a few people anticipated that this would become the American Century. Today, as we prepare to enter the 21st century, we expect that it, too, may belong to the "land of the free and the home of the brave."

Today's Youngsters Follow An Old Path

(Published October 7, 1995)

What does success in life really mean? Is there any preferred course of study or subject that is most important in achieving it?

These are questions which I heard young people in high school and college in this area ask in recent weeks; I believe they are representative of the majority of today's rising generation.

There are those who doubt that this emerging group will measure up to what will be expected of them. To the contrary, these young people are curious, smart, critical, and caring. They and those a few years older have sometimes been referred to as Generation X. A pattern of labeling the young generation in America has evolved; we have had the Lost Generation, the Rock 'n' Roll Generation and others. Also, a few individuals or groups have come to symbolize generations. We have had James Dean, Bob Dylan, the Kennedys, the Rolling Stones, and now Generation X has Brad Pitt.

Today's adults recall their youth nostalgically and express concerns about the younger generation experiencing certain problems for the first time. For example, gangs are frequently in the news. We forget that "West Side Story" was written in the 1950s. While the particulars may change, the substance is similar from generation to generation.

Almost by definition, young people test limits at this time in their lives when there are limitless possibilities. Like prior generations, they express their independence by selecting music, clothing, slang expressions, and hairstyles different from their parents. It is part of the natural process of "growing up." This does not reduce their great potential to positively impact the coming 21st century.

This generation of young people is, I believe, little different from those who have preceded them. However, the skills that they will need to address the changing challenges that they will face will differ in some respects from the skills of their parents. They will need to be computer- and technology-competent, more multi-lingual, more international-oriented, and they will have to manage an overload of information in a time of diminishing privacy.

Generation X will benefit from progress that we have made in reducing the threat of world or nuclear war, in demonstrating that free markets are an effective form of economic activity, and that democracy is the preferred form of legitimate government. They will be burdened by a massive national debt, a damaged environment, and still unresolved racial and gender issues.

On the unlikely chance that members of Generation X will listen to our advice, we may answer one of the questions above by pointing them toward a definition of success that was written at the beginning of this century by Bessie Stanley:

"He or she has achieved success who has lived well, laughed often, and loved much, who has enjoyed . . . the love of little children, who has filled his niche and accomplished his task, who has left the world better than he found it, whether by an improved poppy, a perfect poem, or a rescued soul; who has never lacked appreciation of earth's beauty or failed to express it; who has always looked for the best in others and given them the best he had; whose life was an inspiration; whose memory is a benediction."

James Dean
AP/WIDE WORLD PHOTOS.

DWI Mishap Left Two College Friends Dead

(Published February 22, 1997)

My participation in the events of one Saturday night during the second semester of my freshman year in college is something that I have deeply regretted ever since. I was 18 years old.

The memory is more vivid as spring approaches and whenever I learn about a young person who has been drinking and driving. The story is worth repeating if it helps prevent one accident.

It was Parents' Weekend. A friend drove two of us in his father's car to a party at another school. We all had too much to drink.

While returning to our campus, I was somehow thrown out of the back seat of that convertible as the driver slowed for a curve in the road. The one-car crash and explosion a moment later instantly killed both of my friends. I walked all the way back to my room with some bruises, semi-shocked and dazed.

"He's not here; all three were in the car. We need to decide who will tell his family," were the words of the dean of students that awoke me in an upper bunk bed where he initially did not see me later that morning. I then told him what I recalled of what we had done and asked if he wanted me to speak with my friends' parents. It was one of the worst days of my life

In retrospect, much of the culture of the 1960s reinforced the thought that we were young, cool and immortal. Some of that feeling is synonymous with youth. Fortunately, significant changes in public attitudes and standards occurred later. Organizations formed such as Mothers Against Drunk Driving. Awareness, prevention, and punishment efforts developed, especially seeking to reach young people.

Some important progress has been made with designated driver programs and alcohol-free graduation parties. Currently, proposed legislation in Texas would create a zero-tolerance policy, making it illegal for those under 21 to drive after drinking any amount of alcohol. Such laws are already in place in most other states.

As the only survivor of what happened years ago when drinking and driving were combined, I have a responsibility to write this column. I hope that it makes a contribution to raising consciousness about the menace of drinking and driving and its potential consequences to the lives of all whom may be affected. While I did question my friend who was driving that fatal night, I did not stop him. That is what is required in such a situation.

Perhaps the tragic losses of my two friends and of the futures that they never experienced can serve some purpose; it may be helpful to at least one person who will read this, remember, and neither drink and drive nor allow someone else to make such a potentially fatal mistake.

We've Become Obsessed With The Lives Of Others

(Published March 7, 1998)

"Time (and personal energy) is the coin of your life. It is the only coin that you have. Be careful lest someone else spend it for you."

- Carl Sandburg.

Thinking and acting for one's self is at the essence of a life well lived. Becoming a capable, contributing individual who develops personal abilities as fully as possible has motivated generations of Americans.

From pioneer days to recent times, encouraging educated and independent-thinking citizens has been one of our strengths. As part of our culture, people were often interested in others in a noble way. They were curious about essential aspects of their lives, their life and death, health, significant developments in the passages of life, and other consequential matters.

This positive way of relating to others, and being concerned for their well-being, propelled America to lead the world in volunteerism and unequalled charitable contributions as people provide help and comfort to others.

However, in the last decade of this century, individuality, combined with compassion and community spirit, is being challenged by both excessive commercialism and excessive interest in the excruciating details of others' lives. We have moved from a moderate and balanced position with good judgment in these areas to extremes.

Mass merchandising is overwhelming society. Many people rely on third party endorsements to tell them what to buy and how to live. Recommendations by experts in their spheres of expertise can be helpful, but we now have a galaxy of non-expert celebrity experts.

Commercial objectives have displaced the amateur spirit in many areas, including sports. One reason why the recent Winter Olympics was of less interest than anticipated was the undercurrent of competition for endorsements, and ultimately for money, rather than sport and personal accomplishment.

Overzealous commercialism precludes handling triumph with modesty. Sportsmanship is subordinated to showmanship.

A related distraction from self-development is the excessive demand for personal information about other people. Those formerly general human stories have become absurdly intrusive.

Perhaps, the temporary reduction of critical public issues - like war vs. peace or a recession vs. strong economy - combined with a proliferation of means of communication requiring some kind of content, have contributed to this titillating but pointless phenomenon.

Senseless and silly information about details of others' lives clutters communications and conversations.

The consequences of looking to others as primary sources of personal validation and social identity, and doing so to such excess, need to be considered. The significance of obsessive interest in the lives of others merits reflection. Both undermine a long history of cultural preference for individual decisions, individually made, regarding life's important choices.

It is difficult to substitute others' endorsements and others' lives for our life choices and fulfill ourselves in our personal journey.

"There is only one success - to spend your life in your own way."

- Christopher Morley

Are There Private Ryans In Generation X?

(Published August 28, 1998)

The powerful feature film "Saving Private Ryan" is a graphic depiction of the savagery of war. It is also a tribute to the humanity, decency, and patriotism of the members of the generation who fought World War II.

"Who will take the place of that generation when our country again requires service and sacrifice?" was the question asked at a friend's 50th birthday party in South Texas a few weeks ago.

The person who asked the question was quite skeptical that today's youngsters - Generation X - would measure up to the demands of a war like World War II.

The conversation that evening was prompted, of course, by a concern that our culture has changed.

Our citizens might now emphasize self-satisfaction rather than fulfillment of responsibility and adulation of shallow celebrities rather than true heroes.

"What's in it for me?" has frequently supplanted, "What is my duty?"

The Horatio Alger Association of Distinguished Americans has been interested in these and related issues since its founding over 50 years ago. It's annual report "State of our Nation's Youth" was released recently.

The Horatio Alger report reaffirms that today's young people have values and ideals that are comparable to previous generations.

According to this report, young students are optimistic and positive about the future. They view crime and violence, including issues of school safety, as America's most troubling problem. "Family members rank as the number one source for role models while political leaders rank last."

The youth of today are motivated to be economically successful, but also want to work at making the world a better place.

They seem to understand what may be required of them and are prepared to meet the challenges of their time. They are not unlike prior generations in their basic values and needs as well as their expression of independence.

Generation after generation of Americans have successfully fulfilled their responsibility to meet the challenges of time - military, moral, and economic.

Americans obtained and defended freedom from the Revolutionary War to World War II through today. We achieved victory in the Cold War over communism without atomic annihilation or world-wide conflagration. We worked our way through the Depression and many recessions. We are moving from unequal rights to equal rights.

When the circumstances require it, people emerge within this Republic who exhibit the moral courage and personal strength to overcome adversity and serious threats to our way of life, including terrorism. The nature of what is required may change with the times, but a free society seems best suited to produce the right people and leaders to meet the challenge.

The great 19th century American poet, Walt Whitman, expressed his confidence in the strength and vitality of our nation and his insights ring true as we are about to enter the 21st century: "Democracy, as it exists and practically works in America, with all its threatening evils, supplies a training school for first-class people. It is life's gymnasium, not of good only, but of all."

Whitman describes the coming of age of emerging generations.:
"Have the elder races halted? Do they droop to end their lesson, wearied over there beyond the seas? We take up the task eternal, and the burden and the lesson . . . "

Steven Spielberg
AP/WIDE WORLD PHOTOS.

D-Day Invasion of Nazi Germany's "Fortress Europe"
AP/WIDE WORLD PHOTOS.

Nation Faces Dramatic Changes, Challenges

(Published October 9, 1999)

Thoughts about the significance of, and the possibilities of, the upcoming 21st century and 3rd millennium have overshadowed consideration of a shorter time frame - the next ten years. In our fast-changing world, a decade can bring epochal change.

Political/military developments of great consequence occurred in the 1980's; they included the beginning of the collapse of the former Soviet Union. During the 1990's, exceptional economic achievements propelled the U.S. to a period of historic wealth creation and economic strength. Each of these past two decades had prevailing themes. What will be the dominant theme of the next decade?

Approximately ten years ago, this column suggested the theme of economic resurgence for the 1990's. An October 29, 1988 writing anticipated that domestic economics and economic competition among nations would supplant Cold War military confrontation: "a new Soviet Union may soon exist...and economic competition...among nations...would become more important." A January 27, 1990 column noted: "Enhancing economic strength is the priority...now more than ever," and, "prepare for an acceleration of current trends which will separate economic winners and losers."

As a consequence of the successes of the past twenty years, our military, political, and economic power have placed us in an excellent position. With America's tremendous resources and our historic ideals and values, it is quite possible that social and cultural issues will be priorities during the coming decade - as political/military and economic matters were especially significant in previous decades.

Several factors are in place to propel social and cultural advances. After prolonged material accomplishment, a growing number of people may seek greater significance in their lives from what they do and how they spend their time and capital. What is the purpose of it all? Certainly not just self-indulgence, consumerism, and celebrity-itis.

Private philanthropy is expanding due to the extraordinary accumulation of wealth in this decade. Bill Gates is a recent example of this spirit. Others may be expected to dedicate a portion of their wealth to philanthropic causes. Combined with public funds, the capability to address previously unsolved social issues will become more possible. Motivated people with economic resources can achieve significant objectives and turn great ideas into reality.

Ways in which to enhance the quality of our lives include finding cures for serious diseases, i.e., cancer, advancing education, ensuring fairness in society, and providing appropriately for the needy, the suffering, and the neglected. Our destiny as a nation has been to overcome obstacles in the relentless pursuit of our ideals, i.e., freedom, equality, and justice.

As an eternal optimist about America, I believe that we shall continue to move forward to serve higher purposes and successfully address a number of social and cultural issues just as we prevailed over economic challenges in this decade. While in Corpus Christi in 1989, Dr. Henry Kissinger offered an observation as applicable to the prospect of the coming decade's social and cultural progress as it was to the economics of the 1990's:

"It's not the critics and skeptics who change the world. Great achievements begin as somebody's idea. They are pursued, developed, and brought into being."

Section IV

United States Foreign Policy / International Affairs

We Must Respond To Danger

(Published August 1, 1981)

On most days, like this first of August, we can read this newspaper and learn about the latest suffering in the world's trouble spots - Afghanistan, Lebanon, Cambodia, El Salvador and others. The problems in these places seem remote as we lead our tranquil lifestyle in South Texas. These localized wars and struggles in foreign lands receive passing attention because we had read headlines and articles about one or another of these conflicts for a long time; we are becoming almost insensitive to the most shocking reports. Even though some of the battles are being fought and atrocities committed increasingly closer to a U.S. border, we have not responded with any sense of urgency to this pattern of hostile activity. On the contrary, we have come to accept these struggles with a non-involved, detached attitude.

Many of us have not taken the time to reflect upon the sequence of events that may have a larger meaning in terms of our security. We have not developed and articulated an integrated perspective about what is occurring. Before World War II, the American public and most of the world viewed each event in isolation; people observed curiously and dismissed the significance of individual events.

There is extensive evidence that totalitarian countries and their surrogates have provided support, weapons, and training for a worldwide terrorist network that is dedicated to overthrowing Western democratic societies. These actions should cause concern for peace-loving, freedom-loving people. In combination with troops and agents of oppressive countries, subversives have been operative for many years and grow bolder in their goals. The pattern is ominous.

A number of factors have contributed to our not yet focusing upon this situation. These include: (1) A preoccupation with domestic economic issues. (2) We are only now beginning to move away from our post-Vietnam national psychology. (3) No credible threat in terms of a specific rallying point presenting immediate physical danger has taken place. (4) We have turned increasingly inward to address individual, special interest, and other concerns. We have left open and unanswered a number of questions regarding our military and intelligence priorities.

I believe that we should recognize that a comprehensive view of these "isolated" program areas is appropriate. Our foreign policy should emphasize a strong defense and intelligence component. We need to do what is necessary to dissuade any potential adversary. Our will to confront any real danger to our way of life should be clearly expressed.

We can use more of our country's productive capacity for a period of time to strengthen our national defense and ensure that our children and their children will live in freedom. The administration's defense program is projected to increase the cost. In terms of percentage of Gross National Product devoted to military expenditures, from 5 percent to 7 percent - a lower percentage than the latter 1950's and early 1960's.

To those who may question why a build-up of our national defense capability is really necessary, I would offer Winston Churchill's response to those who asked why the British were arming and fighting the Nazis: he said, "if we stop, you'll find out."

Soviet Policies Unchanging

(Published December 18, 1982)

"Two roads diverged in a wood, and I took the one less traveled by, and that has made all the difference." - Robert Frost

We have much to be thankful for during this holiday season, including the commitment of those who went before us to the less-traveled road. As they created, defended, and built this great country, history was changed as a nation of freedom and opportunity was developed and sustained.

While our country has its problems, they are discussed openly and are resolved within democratic institutional processes. To restrain our primary adversary, we need to maintain these political and economic institutions in sound condition.

That primary adversary is, of course, the Soviet Union. Since Brezhnev's death, there has been speculation and wishful thinking that relations will significantly improve with the new government of Communist Party General Secretary Yuri Andropov. Unfortunately, Soviet totalitarian policies evolve more from consensus ideology and practices of government than from a single national leader.

The new Soviet leader may be initially perceived as different from his predecessors, but his background and experience are rooted in Soviet expansionism and repression. There is little evidence that he will pursue peace as a priority ahead of Communist revolution and exercise of Soviet power. To think that he does not subscribe to Marxist-Leninist-Stalinist-Brezhnevist ideas is to make a serious mistake. While the American Soviet relationship has fluctuated over time, fundamentally the relationship has remained about the same - tense, competitive and threatening. Whenever high hopes existed for détente, they were not fulfilled either by a new Soviet head of state or by the convergence of other factors.

Andropov headed the Soviet secret police, the KGB, since the late 1960's; he was responsible for espionage and internal security. As a senior Communist Party official, he was supportive of, if not an architect of, policies, which included suppression of domestic dissent, crushing the Solidarity movement in Poland,

and invading Czechoslovakia and Afghanistan. Further, he undoubtedly was instrumental in guiding Castro's proxy troops in their many military interventions and in encouraging terrorism and radicalism in the Middle East. He may similarly be expected to pursue Soviet expansionist goals using whatever means he believes will further his objectives. We face a continuing challenge of persuasion on many levels.

This only reinforces the fact that, hope notwithstanding, it is unlikely that substantive changes will take place soon in Soviet destabilizing policies. We need to require meaningful changes, not propaganda and public relations ploys aimed at anxious audiences before altering our policy of containment. The Economist wrote of Brezhnev before his death, "You can't shake hands with a clenched fist."

While the opportunity is clearly there for Andropov to extend or respond to peaceful initiatives, it is unrealistic to expect anything other than cosmetic gestures and necessary accommodations. Whoever may be in Santa Claus clothing next week, one person not to expect is Yuri Andropov - on the less-traveled road.

Our Resolve Must Be Clear

(Published March 5, 1983)

Three weeks ago, the Oxford University Union in England marked the 50th anniversary of a vote among its members in favor of a resolution not to fight for their country under any circumstances. This debating society is a well-known and respected institution: American Rhodes Scholars have been regular observers and frequent participants at their meetings.

That 1933 vote occurred 10 days after Hitler came to power. Winston Churchill called it "a very disgusting and disquieting symptom." Men and women will long discuss whether, and at what point, Hitler could have been stopped. Many of those who supported the resolution later fought and died in the world war that stopped him. The influential Oxford Union, where numerous thoughts and trends have originated, clearly signaled a misleading message.

Through the past half-century, many Oxford Union debaters have argued for positions similar to that 1933 resolution. I remember participating in the early 1960's in a debate at the Colgate University Chapel in upstate New York against the Oxford Union. They contended, "That this House would rather be Red than dead."

It was therefore of interest to learn that three weeks ago, the members of the 1983 Oxford Union overwhelmingly defeated the view, "That this House would not fight for queen and country." It was more than recognition of a terrible mistake exactly a half century earlier. The vote recognized some of today's realities and sent an accurate message.

Last month's debate took place in conditions generally similar to those of 1933. The Western world has been in a global recession. Totalitarian threats exist. A significant peace movement appeals to many. A major difference in the debates, of course, is the experience of those 50 years. Some of history's hard lessons had been learned. Wishful solutions like unilateral disarmament and nuclear freeze were rejected. The error of unconditional non-violence was understood.

One of this year's most moving speakers was a former officer of the union who spoke in favor of the motion in 1933. Max Beloff, now a distinguished teacher and writer of political history described his speech as "an act of atonement" for his vote and a tribute to the memory of a friend who opposed the resolution and then fought and died for freedom.

An important lesson relevant to public policy today in America may be drawn. We want to accurately communicate our resolve even though we have internal debates. In a free country, we encourage diversity. In a democracy, many voices are heard and different views expressed; that is part of our strength in a constructive process. Totalitarian regimes, however, speak only with one voice.

Today's peace movement has its place and its validity. It is supported by many intelligent, patriotic people who care deeply about their country. Nonetheless, I do not believe that there is an effective substitute for preparedness and strength as the basis of sound negotiating strategy when facing totalitarian opponents. No aggressor should be misled as to our intentions and actions as a nation, if challenged.

Our generation seeks peace, but no one should doubt that we are determined not to end up Red, then dead.

Our Will Is The Key To Peace

(Published May 25, 1985)

A few weeks ago, and 10 years after the fall of Saigon, Vietnam veterans marched in the parade that they never had. One million people in New York said "thank you" to those who served in the longest, most frustrating, and controversial war in our country's history. A decade has passed; yet, the war has continued to have a lingering effect upon our national mood and policies. We have been tentative and uncertain in our foreign policy - influenced by post-Vietnam paralysis. Many Americans not only don't want to be the world's policeman, they don't even want to think about how long we can sustain our values as a daily witness to totalitarian and terrorist atrocities around the world.

A few weeks ago, we also celebrated another anniversary - the victory of allied arms over Nazi Germany. The proximity of these two anniversaries leads to certain realizations. We were unquestionably the strongest nation in the world on V-E Day 40 years ago. While other factors contributed, the Vietnam War led to a reduction in our ability to influence world events. As we come to terms with that experience which so divided this country, we have the opportunity to unite as a nation and pursue an effective policy.

This Monday, Memorial Day, when we remember and honor those who gave their lives so that we may live in freedom, let us think about the values for which they fought and the challenges that we currently face. As we emerge from an extended post-Vietnam lack of resolve, it is time to (1) reassess and (2) recommit.

(1) Our democracy permits a branch of Congress to prevent the president from pursuing his national defense policy as recently occurred when the House of Representatives rejected military aid to Nicaragua's Contras.

Totalitarian countries, i.e., the Soviet Union and its agents, are controlled in an oppressive manner with no legislative dissent. A Vietnam weakens our resolve for years. An Afghanistan has no discernible effect on Soviet policies. They relentlessly seek to advance totalitarian communism.

We cannot allow our democratic system to place us at a crippling disadvantage when we deal with totalitarian or terrorist adversaries. We must play the pivotal role in areas of critical importance to us and do what is necessary. Our credibility and ultimate security are at stake. A consensus must be achieved regarding our national interest so that we may project strength in dealing with our single-minded opponents.

Two "negotiations" are currently taking place - in Geneva and among the Contadora nations. The first has the objective of reducing the nuclear arms race and the second the objective of achieving peace in Central America. The goals of each are desirable, but how realistic are the prospects when our adversaries question how prepared we are to act upon our convictions? The line between appeasing and coexisting is a fine one.

The Contadora Group, which has been seeking a settlement in Nicaragua, has been negotiating now for 2-1/2 years - while Communist expansionist intervention continues!

(2) By projecting strength, we would do more to encourage the process to achieve real peace than by sending well-meaning teams to Geneva and Contadora.

Only when our will is not in question can we lessen the probability of major conflict, and properly remember those who are not with us on this Memorial Day because they did what then had to be done.

Will Others Follow This First Step?

(Published November 23, 1985)

Despite months of pre-summit anticipation, and now after a few days of post-summit announcements and analyses, it remains very difficult to believe that this is the time for a fundamental change in U.S.-Soviet relations, including the near-term signing of a meaningful arms control agreement.

It is not that the Soviet's public relations program, including last week's publication of Gorbachev's book, "A Time for Peace," hasn't tried to influence public opinion that more is achievable sooner. It is certainly not that a genuine reduction of the nuclear threat isn't desired by the people of both countries. This is just not the time because we have no current basis on which to trust the Soviet Union, nor its present leader. Whether Gorbachev is a salesman or a statesman to be counted upon is an open question.

The overwhelming publicity about the Reagan-Gorbachev meeting in Geneva, with reports amplifying on every conceivable aspect of the summit, continue each day, including today. It is not easy to cut through the confusion, signals, and counter-signals that often obscure the realities of political and international affairs.

After the last summit in 1979, it was described as having produced (1) historic agreements which were signed, (2) a working relationship between the U.S. president and the Soviet leader, and (3) an atmosphere that would alter history by creating lasting peace. Within weeks, some Soviet brigades settled in Cuba as others invaded Afghanistan. If agreements were unquestionably binding, we would have true confidence in our expectations for peace; however, some people are talented at deception and the facts of history show that they simply cannot be trusted.

Napoleon and Hitler signed agreements with the Russians calling for peaceful relations; they then invaded the Soviet Union. In a twisted way, the Soviet Union has adopted the tactics of its former aggressors by signaling peaceful intentions, or entering into agreements, and then proceeding to implement its expansions and totalitarian goals - irrespective of its commitments to the contrary. Post-World War II history until this week amply documents this pattern.

This week's summit could be the first step in achieving a new era in the relationship between our country and the Soviet Union. Both countries have ample incentives to reach understandings and accommodations on many levels. We both have sufficient domestic problems to which resources could be applied that will otherwise go toward escalating defense budgets. Pointing in a positive direction is this week's improvement in communication and promise for future progress toward verifiable, meaningful agreements.

Hope notwithstanding, the essential aspects of the complicated issues that separate the two countries were not altered this week. The lofty goals that pre-summit speculation encouraged remained elusive. We continue to want to believe that their realization is foreseeable.

If the Soviets are serious in reaching solid accords on real issues, then this may be the season for substantial progress in superpower relations. On the other hand, if the Soviets are engaged in an exercise of cynical publicity, then this is not yet the season for the beginning of a genuine peace process. We shall have to continue to watch closely to see whether this is the time that latter-half 20th Century history began to change - or whether this week will be noteworthy only as the one before Thanksgiving, 1985.

U.S. Should Focus On Mexico, Instead Of Europe

(Published July 5, 1986)

John Adams prophesied, after he signed the Declaration of Independence in 1776, "July 4th will be celebrated by succeeding generations . . . with pomp and parade, with shows . . . and illuminations from one end of this continent to the other, from this time forward for evermore."

This year's Independence Day festivities coincided with a celebration in New York Harbor of the restoration of the Statue of Liberty that was given to our country by France 100 years ago. Beginning with French support for the American Revolution, there has been a close relationship between the two countries. In this century, we saved France as a nation twice, and then restored its economy after World War II.

Ironically, notwithstanding all of this holiday weekend's ceremonies and speeches, significant differences in policy objectives and in respective perceptions have recently emerged among our country, France, and other countries in Western Europe. The failure of a number of Western European countries, with the one exception of Great Britain, to respond positively to our request for cooperation in our military response to Libyan state-supported terrorism has highlighted many strategic and foreign policy questions for us. Those many countries that refused advised that their national self-interest and priorities required their response.

We, too, should assess our current national self-interest and reorder our priorities so that countries south of our border, led by Mexico, receive some of the attention and resources that have been concentrated upon Western Europe. Our government's largest foreign expenditures continue to be in Western Europe; they are primarily military. The absolute dollar commitment is very large. Countries there can afford to increase their contribution as ours is reduced.

Last week, Secretary of State Shultz observed that New Zealand had not cooperated, as we should expect from an ally. As a result he stated that, "we part company as friends, but we part company . . . " This appears to be an appropriate time to begin to take a comparable position regarding the extensive financial and people resources that we devote to the countries of Western Europe. We need not necessarily end, just reduce, our commitment level. We would remain friends with those countries, but our resources would be focused more according to America's increasing priority to control its border and truly recognize the importance of the problem/opportunity that is so geographically close to us.

The news and editorial pages of this newspaper continue to inform us of the many problems in Mexico and of their significance for this country. Deep political, economic, institutionalized corruption and other issues require resolution that can only come from within Mexico; there are some indications that quiet pressures are being applied to return some of Mexico's flight capital to help build that nation's economy. This needs to be intensified. More positive incentive may come from the prospect of a closer partnership between the United States and Mexico in mutual self-interest. Mexico needs more than short-term credit extensions. We must assure the long-term security of our southern border and the stability of our neighbor.

Hopefully, present and succeeding generations of people in both countries will benefit from results achieved by addressing Mexico as a priority area, and by shifting foreign policy priorities and resources accordingly.

Tibet Is The Real Litmus Test Of Openness In China

(Published November 7, 1987)

As international events unfold, one former teacher's words provide continuing insight: he is Dr. John Stoessinger of San Antonio's Trinity University. He instilled in us recognition of "the divergence between the images that we entertain of world affairs . . . and international realities as they actually are."

One current example of this concept concerns the People's Republic of China. In recent years China has been experimenting with economic and cultural freedom to address internal economic problems. Their initiatives have been followed by the Soviet Union's glasnost.

Increasing contact, communication, and the prospect of a large new market have led us to become somewhat enamored with China. China's apparent reforms have reinforced our hope that the world's most populated country could be shifting from Mao's communism to Deng and Zhao's perhaps more benevolent Marxism - with perhaps a hint of democratic values.

Then we learn of the events beginning in late September in Tibet. We reflect upon Tibet since China invaded that isolated country in 1950 and wonder whether China is changing for real or not.

Tibet was a unique civilization; it had a highly evolved valuable culture that was the sole repository of original Buddhism. Their philosophic, medical, psychological, and artistic perspective and understanding attracted world interest and respect.

What took well over 1,300 years to build, China has essentially destroyed in less than forty years. More than one million people perished in work camps (one-sixth of the population) and 6,254 monasteries were destroyed; five were left. Two-thirds of its original territory was annexed by Chinese provinces with one part remaining as the Tibet Autonomous Region.

A systematic, repressive destruction of Tibetan district identity and culture has taken place. Tibet has become an apartheid society with native Chinese being relocated into Tibet to outnumber and eventually replace native Tibetans. While exact figures are difficult to obtain, it is estimated that political prisoners number in the tens of thousands. Even Aleksandr Solzhenitsyn described the communist rule in Tibet as "more brutal and inhumane than any other communist regime in the world."

Military, strategic and natural resource requirements will keep Tibet as part of China; within that framework, nonetheless, the terms of domination are of interest to the world.

The U.S. Congress passed a formal resolution condemning China's abuses in Tibet in June of this year. Tibet's exiled spiritual and political leader, the Dalai Lama, spoke before the Congress' human rights caucus on Sept. 21. He proposed a five-point program, including respecting basic rights and freedoms. The Chinese immediately herded 15,000 people into a stadium in Tibet's capital, Lhasa. Political obedience was taught by sentencing eight Tibetans to prison, and publicly executing two others.

Decades of Chinese communist repression had still not eliminated Tibetan spirit. Demonstrations ensued which left many Tibetans dead and injured. The Chinese authorities then expelled all foreign journalists from Tibet.

The world now awaits information from and about Tibet. Will the Chinese permit the spiritually committed Tibetans to practice their beliefs and traditions? Will a totalitarian solution continue to be applied to a desire for human freedom reform in Tibet? Will one of the two major communist countries of the world permit limited freedom only when it perceives no threat? When vital interests may be at risk, should we expect brutal totalitarian methods?

The answers to the questions will help us all distinguish images from realities in today's China.

Dalai Lama (speaking to U.S. Congress about Chinese in Tibet)
AP/WIDE WORLD PHOTOS.

Global Economic Changes Have Major Implications

(Published March 12, 1988)

There is a cost to achieving significant positive change.

History offers few examples of meaningful transformation being achieved without considerable pain and adjustment over time - in almost all aspects of life. One sphere where this currently is relevant is economic; world, national, and local changes are taking place with attendant challenges.

On a national level, public Corporate America is being transformed. During this decade, an active, well-financed market for control of major U.S. corporations has developed. The escalating globalization of industry and finance, deregulation, the creation of pools of capital seeking investments, rapid technological change, and other factors fuel this market. Recently, the weakened dollar and lower interest rates intensify the action.

Corporate restructurings, whether resulting from takeovers, leverage buy-outs, recapitalizations, spin-offs, or other forms, are premised on values not being recognized and realized in the pre-change era. What is distinctive today is that the demand for performance comes from so many directions - the emergence of concentrated capital in public and institutional funds, international currency relationships, bold raiders, shrewd traders, and powerful financiers. The underlying forces are nonetheless creating permanent structural change to respond to the unique conditions of our time.

The intense competition for the right and responsibility to control and manage substantial corporate resources has many implications.

On the negative side, there have been excesses. An efficient market for capital allocation and corporate control has messy and imperfect assets. Insider trading, greenmail, and techniques to entrench and enrich poor-performing managements are but some of the problems. Restructuring on this scale frequently involves real costs in human suffering, as jobs are lost.

However, there are positive aspects of the tidal wave of change in Corporate

America. Recent studies have shown that a decade of corporate restructurings have produced many better managed companies with less waste and more effective asset utilization. Shareholder values are being maximized and jobs are created. While unemployment remains a serious problem in some areas, more people are working than at any time in American history. American businesses are growing as better management and more focused business units meet domestic and international competitive tests by operating efficiently.

The restructuring of Corporate America is part of a larger process of global economic change, with its national and regional implications. The formerly status quo is now status change; that change is taking place at a fast pace throughout much of our service, industrial, and financial sectors. The standards to survive, and perhaps succeed, are constantly tougher.

As Corporate America recognizes the heightened standards of performance required today, the changes necessitated will be structural and lasting. Those prepared and capable to implement them are obtaining effective control of massive resources. As those corporations become more competitive, they will sell more of their products, export more, and employ more people. Only then will the short-term pain and cost be replaced by longer-term opportunity and confidence.

Policymakers Need To Stand Back, And Take The Long View

(Published October 29, 1988)

Every now and then, we should look beyond the immediate future to get another perspective on the present. Sometimes, being far away provides special insight.

For the past several years, I have visited with a friend in Chicago after his return from trips to Nepal. He spends weeks trekking through that country with no communication whatsoever with the outside world - often in villages where people live exactly as their ancestors did centuries ago. Recently, he returned and discussed some ideas, which resulted from being far away and doing some original thinking.

Those who have correctly anticipated and prepared for fundamental change have been those who led in those spheres of change as they occurred. For example, in business, those who recognized early the restructuring of Corporate America through mergers and leveraged buy-outs have led in this area through much of this decade.

In the sphere of international relations, too, great opportunity awaits those who have foresight and prepare themselves accordingly. If President Reagan is correct and we are truly seeing "the receding tide of totalitarianism," what appears to be happening in the Soviet Union could have far-reaching implications.

Seventy-one years of history should be enough to cause us to be cautious in our acceptance of a "new" Soviet Union. Reducing our strong defenses - either physical or mental - is not prudent in the near future. However, the near future can be a short time in this rapidly shifting world.

It may be constructive to consider international relations using an assumption (however remote) that a "new" Soviet Union may soon exist; if so, the goals of that nation may shift away from military priorities in favor of economic goals and tactics. Economic competition and related alliances among nations would become even more important. Our foreign policy has focused upon containing the Soviet Union militarily for most of the lives of those reading this column. Should there be a real basis to change this dominant policy, economics-based foreign policy (ecopolitics) could complement geo-military policy (geopolitics) as strategic imperatives for the next generation.

International economic trends, combined with a reordering of priorities that would result from a "new" Soviet Union (they could even change their name - Allegis is available!), could shift traditional alliances dramatically. This is already underway in Europe. The 1992 internal economic unification of the European Community is a tangible version of a shift based upon ecopolitics.

Were the superpowers to truly move toward more demilitarized economies, Europe's strategic interests could be redefined. While Europe and the United States share democratic values and common heritage, those factors may not assure an alliance when economic interests diverge.

Japan need not change its focus; its priorities were directed toward ecopolitics decades ago. An economically directed Soviet Union, with its large oil and gas deposits could play a different role in Japan beyond the immediate future.

Third World relations may also experience interesting dynamics. Mexico and Canada would become more important priorities of our foreign policy. Further, in areas where we "tilt" toward certain countries because of their military value to us in containing the "old" Soviet Union, we may want to revisit our policies. For example, our "tilt" toward Pakistan is based in part upon geopolitics. Under ecopolitical priorities, a re-analysis would be appropriate in light of India's production and consumption potential.

Past formulas and alliances, which worked during the mid-20th century may require revision as the 21st century approaches. Bold and creative thinking and leadership are needed for the rapidly changing political, military, and economic environment of our times.

By thinking about these possibilities today, we can begin to formulate policies, which assure the continuation of our country's leadership and strength in, and beyond, the immediate future.

Crisis Reveals New World Order, With The U.S. At The Top

(Published September 8, 1990)

Considerable time will pass before all of the implications of the Persian Gulf crisis are known and understood. Nonetheless, it may be useful to consider some working conclusions drawn from the facts to date.

Saddam Hussein believed that no country would stop him when he invaded Kuwait on his way to Saudi Arabia. He was almost correct. He miscalculated the resolve of the Bush administration and our country. If the United States had not taken decisive action in early August, what impact would a United Nations debate have had upon this ruthless, ambitious despot who would then control almost one-half of the world's oil? Not much.

The Iraqi invasion of Kuwait and the threat to Saudi Arabia made it clear that only one country in the world had the strength and the will to defend its interests and deter aggression; the United States. Some of our allies in Europe and Japan have subsequently provided secondary and, except for Britain and France, largely symbolic military support. The United States stood alone when the crisis was most acute in those first weeks after Aug. 2. This cannot help but lead to significant reassessment of international relations and recognition of the undisputed global pre-eminence of the United States, especially in times of crisis. Several countries, which have recently been lionized for their economic accomplishments and perceived as world leaders, were found wanting when a formidable challenge was faced. There may be a re-ordering of the status quo ante accordingly.

President Bush was very successful in marshalling broad and deep support for his policies at the United Nations and elsewhere. However, no one should lose sight of the fact that implementation of diplomatic efforts through the United Nations' "collective action" and "respect for international law," became viable options only because of the decisive exercise of strength and power by this country. In what is still a dangerous world, a strong military capability and the will to use it are what provide the framework for international legal and institutional mechanisms to be relevant.

The ensuing United Nations support was made possible only by the end of the Cold War. This was the first time that the Soviet Union and our country cooperated in a matter of this magnitude. The nature of further understandings or lack of such may well be determinative in the resolution of this crisis.

Another conclusion is that sound judgment was exercised in intervening in this situation. There are other trouble spots and conflicts in the world - Cambodia, Liberia, Kashmir and others where we have not become similarly committed. Several factors existed in the Mideast, which required our action.

One was the importance of oil to the world's economies. Another was the prospect that aggression by an ambitious Saddam Hussein would be unchecked and that his territorial success would lead to greater instability in a vital area that is already unstable.

A third was that Saudi Arabia has supported our economic interests in the past; the corollary is that we protect it if threatened. A fourth was that our unhesitating response confirmed that we could be relied upon to fulfill our part of explicit or implicit agreements. Finally, the United States has an interest in stopping any tyrant before his destructive and threatening capability gives him the weapons to be an even greater menace to world order.

These are some of the essential issues which have emerged from the current crisis thus far; we cannot permit our current clear sense of national purpose to become obscured by the ever-troubling sandstorms of the Mideast. We cannot be held hostage too long by being pre-occupied with this situation as we have serious domestic problems that are long overdue to be addressed. We may maintain some military position in the Mideast, which we have been preparing for anyway, but this force, cannot dominate our agenda in the 1990's as another "expeditionary force" did in Vietnam in the 1960's. As sound and firm judgment was used in involving our country in the Persian Gulf crisis, equally sound and firm judgment must be used to resolve this and extricate the United States in a timely and effective manner.

China And U.S.: Do We Understand Each Other?

(Published March 2, 1996)

"Chinese Association for International Understanding/Council Member/ Beijing" - read the cards of two representatives of China with whom I had dinner in Chicago a few weeks ago.

Our host was a leading entrepreneur who also invited several other guests, including an English executive who was a former member of Lady Margaret Thatcher's Cabinet.

The Chinese had requested the meeting to encourage investment in their country and to learn what some people think about China. Do we understand China the way it believes it should be understood?

China's potential impact on international life is, of course, enormous. With one-fifth of the world's population, an extraordinary history, and a current puzzle of social, political, and economic contradictions, it is an uncertain nation in transition; to what is the open question.

The discussion focused upon our lack of confidence in their respect for human rights and their system of law.

Unelected authorities and bosses rule rather than laws. America's largest fast-food operator had a valuable lease terminated at will in China recently. Financial information services were "allowed" until one day when they were abruptly "not allowed" earlier this year. The promise of China's markets is offset by the risk of unpredictable action by its government.

I recalled being in Hong Kong in 1984 as a part of delegation from Corpus Christi led by then Mayor Luther Jones when the first of what became many businesses there announced their departure. The reason was Hong Kong's anticipated 1997 return to China and exceptional concern then as now about China's legal system. While China says that it wants to be a responsible world power, it frequently does not act like one.

We spoke about opportunities as well as many other problems regarding China. While we found common ground in a number of areas, the differences were considerable.

The Chinese representatives were very well educated and informed, engaging, and impressive as individuals. They spoke about America with great respect and desire for our assistance in becoming a developed country.

What was most significant for us was their consistent response to our questions. "Our priority is to maintain stability in a country of 1.2 billion people," was their position. They spoke of 70 to 80 million people "wandering" in China at all times. While there is regional diversity, a strong, centralized direction and control is a necessity for "stability." They said, "neither we nor the world want an unstable China."

They expressed the view that China deserves unique treatment and understanding from the world because of their previous suffering.

From the Opium War to the more recent Japanese occupation and the oppression of Mao Zedong's Cultural Revolution, they see themselves as victims of modern history. Accordingly, while it is balancing various considerations while transforming, China should be excused and not held accountable by others' standards for its actions. China should be "understood."

We concluded that part of the problem of relating to, and interfacing with, China, is that many of its people do not view as serious a number of matters that we see as very real problems.

Differences in values, perceptions, and experiences remain formidable. One hopes that dialogue, communication, and interaction will be effective in encouraging China to fulfill its positive promise.

The stakes are high, as the challenge of China's future is one that will likely have a significant impact on the world as it enters the 21st century.

Mao Zedong
AP/WIDE WORLD PHOTOS.

NATO Needs To Do Some Soul-Searching

(Published May 1, 1999)

Walking in Washington last weekend among memorials to some of the most outstanding presidents in our nation's history, and to those courageous, great patriots who fought our country's wars, was thought-provoking. It was inspiring to remember the actions taken by those heroes in the face of the adversity of their time.

My visit to our nation's capital coincided with continuing revelations of barbarities in Kosovo and with ceremonies commemorating the 50th anniversary of the founding of NATO.

NATO was created to respond to a potential life-threatening challenge to its member states. With the developments of recent years, there is no longer such a massive threat. The dangers and issues faced by NATO have changed.

The Balkans have been the site of brutality throughout this decade. Stopping these atrocities is clearly consistent with building a better world, but are significant national interests of NATO's member states seriously threatened? NATO's structure was not originally designed to respond to such limited crises and regional wars. It took considerable time even to decided to use air power. In the democracies that comprise NATO, sensitivity to domestic politics, including casualties and POW's, is significant, and frequently delays decisions.

This raises the foreign policy issue that is faced by every American generation - do we only commit our armed forces for a clear threat to our national interest, or do we act on the humanitarian values of the good, decent people of America?

Throughout our history, we have fluctuated between idealistic policies such as Woodrow Wilson's "making the world safe for democracy," and the *realpolitik* of Richard Nixon/Henry Kissinger which emphasizes the protection of our direct economic and territorial interests.

In evaluating approaches to implement our and NATO's objectives more effectively, consideration might be given to new options. Perhaps we should agree in advance that contiguous, front-line countries have the primary responsibility for providing ground troops. Accordingly, the Europeans should provide ground soldiers in Kosovo.

Another option might be to create a NATO Foreign Legion to conduct such operations. This would be a modification of the Foreign Legion of France which provided a military capability for foreign wars. A NATO Foreign Legion could be comprised of volunteers, or volunteer units of standing armies, who are ready to act in those situations in which NATO has an interest, including humanitarian, but no country has compelling cause to order large numbers of its men and women in harm's way.

While countries, including ours, may not have traditional strategic interests at stake, we do have substantial compassion and dedication to helping those in genuine need.

Humanitarian concerns are the core of American values and priorities. They are at the essence of who and what we are as a people.

As the world's only superpower and greatest democracy, we should take a lead role in re-creating a multi-national alliance to be more effective in the coming century. We have a responsibility to all who have sacrificed before us to use our strength and power for higher purposes than being the world's largest market for cell phones and television commercials. We have a responsibility and moral imperative to help; we need to decide how much.

"All that is necessary for the triumph of evil is that good men do nothing." - Edmund Burke.

President Richard Nixon
AP/WIDE WORLD PHOTOS.

Section V

United States Government – Economic Policy And Other Public Issues

We Must Face Two Challenges

(Published October 25, 1980)

Those of us who remember the 1950's, '60's and early '70's remember a time of confidence, of national strength and economic growth, and a period of certain policies in one's home and in the country's domestic and foreign programs. We participated individually in a sense of being that was reflected in our leadership position as a nation.

In the recent past, a proliferation of single issue and special interest considerations have had an undue influence on our national life and institutions. That influence has been positive in some ways but it has often preceded consideration of our national interest and now tests our will and ability to focus.

While recognizing the genuine importance of a broad range of issues, I would observe that there are two predominant problems affecting the country now, the successful resolution of which will have a significant bearing upon our ability to appropriately respond to other valid concerns. Those are: (1) our ability to implement a foreign policy based upon a sound national defense, and (2) our ability to control inflation and provide a continuing basis of confidence in our economy and currency. If these two issues are not addressed successfully, a victory by any particular special interest group on its narrow point of concern will be a hollow triumph.

With regard to No. 1, the United States must have a comprehensive policy and capability to deal with international realities, which are increasingly unstable. A commitment to defense beyond campaign rhetoric would imply the will to use it. When others see that our position is firm, it will lessen the probability of conflict and improve the opportunity to achieve someday a meaningful détente.

With regard to No. 2, a "reindustrialization" and "degovernmentalization" program is needed. Many governmental expenditures result from special constituencies obtaining a "larger piece of the bureaucratic pie." The answer of the government has led, paradoxically, to the current problem of the government. Budget deficits are a large contributor to our inflationary problem. The federal government has apparently been operating on the premise that continuing budget deficits can only be repaid by making currency less valuable. We need to stop pursuing short-term, narrow objectives and respond with measures that assure a long-run healthy economic system both to directly reduce the inflationary spiral and to affirm a standard.

Elections should determine directions in decisive ways .. 1980 is a year for fundamentals. In order to perpetuate the American democratic way of life in the viable dimensions of the final score of years in the 20th Century, it will be up to individual Americans to meet the challenge and the burdens of a complex struggle - with liberty and our way of life at stake.

Ralph Waldo Emerson told us over a century ago what type of people the American democratic style needed to perpetuate itself: "Men and women of original perception and original action . . . men of elastic, men of moral mind, who can live in the moment and take a step forward."

Now is the time to decide, first, to vote on Nov. 4, and, then, to consider the central importance of two issues at the core of our national circumstance.

Survey Takes Aim At Waste

(Published July 24, 1982)

A unit of the federal government spent $6,000 to prepare 17 pages of instructions on how to buy Worcestershire sauce. Another paid $75,298 for a study on why bowlers, hockey fans and pedestrians smile. The interstate highway system had a $100 billion cost overrun due to mismanagement, delays, and confusion.

These examples of federal government waste received the "Golden Fleece" award from Sen. William Proxmire of Wisconsin, who has been publicizing these activities for many years.

Most of us are familiar with the loss of discipline and accountability in the federal governmental process - symbolized by budget deficits for 13 consecutive years and a national debt that exceeds over $1 trillion. Widespread endorsement of a proposed constitutional amendment requiring a balanced federal budget is one of many responses to the situation.

I became familiar with another response firsthand at a meeting with President Reagan in the East Room of the White House on Thursday one week ago. The president discussed "an important step" in the direction of reversing uncontrollable and runaway government spending - "the private sector survey on cost control in the federal government."

The survey, created by presidential order on June 30, is directed by business executives, plus representatives from the labor and academic communities. This nonpartisan, nonpolitical, and privately funded review of all departments, agencies, and other entities of the executive branch of government is to result in reduced federal spending. The president seeks to "use the ideas, creativity and energy of private sector citizens to contribute to a more effectively managed and operated government." The executive committee, appointed by the president, is charged with searching out waste and inefficiency in the federal government; it is divided into 35 task forces to implement this effort.

This is the first total review of the workings of the executive branch of the federal government since the second Hoover Commission during the

1950's. It is the first comprehensive effort to reduce the cost of operating the federal government in U.S. history!

The changing of processes and procedures that yield most painfully to change will not be easy. Nevertheless, obtaining cost-effective and efficient operations in the executive branch of the federal government would have a tremendous positive impact for the whole country. It is one part of a program to reduce federal spending which will reduce federal capital requirements. That should lead to significantly lower interest rates, with among other benefits, an increase in available jobs.

The executive committee of this "top priority" survey is to report to the president by the end of this year. He stressed the importance of time. The federal government spends $83 million an hour - the interest on our national debt for an hour is almost $11 million.

As I left the meeting, I had a very positive feeling that a real effort was underway. I felt confident that results would be obtained. Everyone in the historic room concurred and was motivated by the president's words, "It is simply not right for us to squander money for which our children and grandchildren will be held accountable."

Three Decisions - Three Jolts

(Published September 3, 1983)

When the second-most powerful person in America, as viewed by many, resigned earlier this year, it was stunning news. This summer, the youngest general in the U.S. Army when appointed to that rank in 1981, resigned. Last week, our senior senator, who is an important committee chairman, announced that he would not stand for re-election next year. We all expected 1984 to provide national political headlines. We did not anticipate this premature arrival of tomorrow.

First, Senate Majority Leader Howard Baker announced his retirement from the Senate. He has since recommended significant changes in the way Congress is structured. He does not believe that professional politicians, subject to continuous interest group pressure, can act with self-discipline. He encourages changing the system to provide that non-paid citizens comprise the House and Senate. They should have a private career, spend less time in Washington, and get more accomplished by focusing upon major issues. Baker continues to articulate ideas to control or limit the public sector and the legislative process; this is needed to maintain political freedom and an economy capable of sustained growth.

Gen. Peter Dawkins, former All-American on an undefeated Army football team, Heisman trophy winner, Rhodes Scholar, decorated Vietnam veteran, and expected future Army chief of staff, personifies an American hero. Gen. Dawkins stated his desire to enter the private sector and then address "challenges that are very compelling" to him "involving the resolution to some of the great problems of our times."

Finally, Sen. John Tower said that he was "burned-out," and wanted to return to the private sector and to teaching. As the most recent surprise, we want to learn more about the thoughts and views that affected his decision.

Considerable speculation has occurred, and may be expected, regarding the implications of these individual decisions. Each decision was, of course, personal and complex. Nonetheless, there are certain common denominators of these three events that are of interest. According to present information, each was a decision by an exceptionally powerful person to voluntarily relinquish his position. Each was at, or near, the top of the public institution of which he had been a part for most of his adult life. Each had served his country with dedication and was not part of the "give-me" generation. Further, each was directly engaged with many of the issues that are most important to us.

Perhaps it was this last fact that made most of our initial reactions to these resignations ones of concern. We complain about the federal government's ineffectiveness as an institution to respond to serious problems with urgency and efficiency. Indeed, it is often ineffective as evidenced by the necessity of appointing special commissions to deal with significant problems, i.e., Social Security, Central America, and federal government cost control. We assumed that those at the top would continue day-after-day to operate in that frustrating environment. With their departure, more may be demanded of us, including working for a change in the way the government operates; let us consider the legislative reforms urged by Sen. Baker. In no field are we as insufficiently vigorous in innovation, so unwilling or unable to address serious issues directly as we are in our national legislative process.

If, in fact, the resignations of Sens. Baker and Tower and Gen. Dawkins are a final departure from public life of these valuable and talented people, then the nation has suffered a loss. On the other hand, if their moves to the private sector provide them with new vigor and vision and they later return to some form of public service, we shall all be the beneficiaries.

It's A Time Of National Paradoxes

(Published March 31, 1984)

Reading, or re-reading literary classics can be rewarding in many ways. On one level, observations about life in different times and places provide a perspective for today. For instance,

"it was the best of times, it was the worst of times, it was the age of wisdom, it was the age of foolishness."

Written more than a century ago, these words from Charles Dickens' "A Tale of Two Cities" seem as appropriate today as then. As simultaneous and contradictory conditions existed then, they do now. Let's consider a few subjects where we may understandably have a feeling of ambivalence on this spring day.

• The national economy has never been stronger with more people employed - over 105 million - than ever before in our history. Capital investment is increasing and more employment opportunities are being created. Inflation is in low, single-digits. Our growing economy is demonstrating strength and productive capacity.

At the same time, our national debt and the annual deficits incurred in operating the federal government are staggering. With our high employment, we still have many people who cannot find a job. Also, the international banking system has monumental problems; rescheduling and other techniques postpone the recognition that many of these foreign debts are not going to be paid.

• Most of us have grown up in a strong, free America that seeks to do that which is right based on respect for personal dignity. As a nation, we have been committed to containing totalitarian communism for 40 years. We have been firm in our opposition to international terror.

However, the combination of certain personalities, events, and legislation, i.e., the War Powers Act, has led to a sense of foreign policy hesitation and confusion. The executive branch and the Congress seem to have as many differences within themselves, and with each other, as they do with other nations. Everyone in Washington is trying to be the secretary of state. We seem tentative and uncertain of our convictions and goals.

• We perceive ourselves as a nation of doers, and, for the most part, we are. Our energies have traditionally been mobilized to identify and solve problems. We communicate and repeat facts about a number of important concerns. Ultimately, we begin to act positively to address some of them, like the education of our children and the recognition of their teachers.

However, we delay until the eleventh hour focusing upon matters that are well-known and require attention, such as our insolvent Medicare system and our ineffective immigration policy. We don't seem to accomplish as much as we are capable.

Significant progress in resolving some of these paradoxes may occur as a result of the election this fall. Hopefully, when we elect or re-elect a president and a Congress, a coherent vision and policy will be voted upon and a mandate provided that can be implemented.

In the meantime, we can be reassured that no other people at any other point in time had more answers than we do to complicated, contradictory aspects of life and public policy. In the meantime, also, we can turn to reading a comedy.

This Is Time To Ponder Great Issues

(Published December 15, 1984)

"What is life? It is the flash of a firefly in the night . . . it is the little shadow which runs across the grass and loses itself in the sunset."

Last words of Crowfoot, a great hunter of the Blackfoot.

If there is a time to be conscious of living, it is during the forthcoming holiday season. Most of the year, we are preoccupied with the *ch* factor in our lives - chasing, changing, and choosing.

For the next few weeks, however, we shall be with family and friends, sifting our present lives through our remembered past, and observing the traditions that we have known since childhood. The holidays usually create great memories and offer some quiet time for perspective. Some personal observations even lead to New Year's resolutions and good intentions to fulfill them.

In addition to personal reflection, this is an appropriate time to think about the most important of public concerns. Following are my choices regarding most important issues as we approach a new year, 1985, with some observations about each:

1. Corpus Christi - encourage economic development. We have a solid economic base. Nonetheless, we need to diversify further to ensure the community resources to support a high quality of life. We need to continue to coordinate our economic development activities. We should build upon the unified effort to attract a Navy homeport as an excellent example of organizing and focusing our strengths.

Our best asset is the people of this community. The producer of "Legends" said that he chose Corpus Christi as the location for this feature film not only for geographical reasons, but because "this is a city that has people who really care."

2. The United States - reduce the budget deficit and pass new tax legislation. The reduction of the budget deficit is not a Republican or Democrat, liberal or conservative issue; it is an American issue that, if not

corrected, will affect the foundation of this country and the lives and livelihood of our children and grandchildren. Federal government expenditures must be reduced by implementing a number of measures, including the principal recommendations of the Grace Commission, freezes, and cuts in expenditures in many programs.

It is important, also, to pass new tax legislation not only to achieve more fairness and simplicity, but also to remove uncertainty. With all of the proposed legislation, including that from the U.S. Treasury, people will be reluctant to commit capital to new investment until they know the tax structure.

3. The world - stop Soviet expansionism and terrorism. The Soviet drive for territory and influence continues - Eastern Europe, Afghanistan, Ethiopia, Southeast Asia, Cuba, Nicaragua, and who knows what nation is next? Arms negotiations have historically proven to be useful to the Soviets in disarming the West as they cheat and advance their national objective of world domination.

While we all hope to reduce the nuclear threat and the arms race, it will take a change in Soviet objectives and character to achieve real peace. A second Russian Revolution may be necessary which will produce leaders that have concerns, goals, and values compatible with our own.

One New Year's wish for all of us who cherish our freedom to share is for Soviet totalitarianism to pass from history quicker than a firefly's flash.

Litigation Has Turned Into Lottery

(Published February 8, 1986)

During a recent discussion regarding the prospects for a national or state lottery, someone noted that we already have both - in the form of current tort litigation. Imaginative plaintiffs and their attorneys are reaping staggering windfalls. Like a lottery, the bill for these excessive awards in this high stakes activity is paid by someone. We all pay in terms of higher insurance premiums and higher prices for virtually everything. Individuals, businesses, cities, hospitals, school districts, and anyone else who may be held financially responsible, are being affected.

Our legal system for helping those who have been seriously injured obtain legal redress has moved too far toward favoring the plaintiff. At least one prominent trial attorney would argue that the defendant was favored years ago. Nonetheless, the chief justice of the United States has told the American Bar Association several times recently that there are too many lawyers, that they encourage people to be too litigious, and that our judicial processes are being abused; the court system is significantly overburdened. A recent Roper poll showed that only one-third of Americans believe that our current tort system is fair. Rather than having confidence in reasonable, predictable standards, people believe that where a claim is litigated and how effective the attorneys are determines the result.

In many instances, jury awards are far out of line with a defendant's actual culpability. One defendant was ordered to pay $260,000 and $1,500 monthly to a man who was injured while robbing a school. The threat of excessive jury verdicts forces many defendants to settle even when they are not at fault; the legal shakedown has emerged. The money involved is leading to a redistribution of wealth from those who produce goods and services, and their insurers, to those who claim injury and their lawyers.

Current practices threaten the very foundation of the U.S. economy. Virtually all producers of goods and services are being severely impacted by the soaring costs or unavailability of liability insurance. Left unrestrained, the insurance market problems will lead to plant closings, reduction of medical and other professional services, restrictions in innovation and constructive risk-taking, and higher prices for all consumers. Ultimately, we shall bear the full economic, cultural and human cost of supporting the earning of money through "gravy-train litigation" rather than encouraging the production of goods or services.

The current crisis with respect to availability of liability insurance also threatens the continued service by capable people in responsible positions. Only last week, the former name law partner of Texas Supreme Court Chief Justice John Hill resigned from the board of a Dallas-based public company. The day he resigned coincided with the expiration of that company's officers' and directors' liability policy.

A search for solutions should include federal product liability reform such as that being developed by a U.S. Senate committee which will shortly hold hearings on proposed corrective legislation. Limits should be placed on the amount of damages that can be awarded. Fault, rather than strict liability, should be the basis for responsibility. Alternatives to litigation, such as the Nueces County Dispute Resolution Center, should be encouraged and supported. Further recommendations need to be developed by knowledgeable people.

Current excesses have created a lottery-like zeal. Many plaintiffs and their attorneys are cashing in on winning tickets for staggering sums. Unless constructive change is realized, we are all going to have to continue this unintended lottery.

It's A New World Out There And U.S. Must Adapt To Survive

(Published January 27, 1990)

Exactly 15 months ago today, this writer communicated some thoughts here suggesting "that a new Soviet Union may soon exist." Also, that "economic competition . . . among nations . . . would become more important," and that future leaders in this economic arena would be "those who had correctly anticipated and prepared for fundamental change."

Examining the United States' situation in a world environment where economic strength is increasingly the standard of national power seems appropriate. To reach as many people as possible in this era of MTV and visual aids, some have suggested that the message be put to music or written with an eyecatcher so as to be both entertaining and enlightening.

Economic considerations, perhaps more than any other, have been the powerful shaping forces throughout history. One of the reasons that the Soviet Union and Eastern Europe are now undergoing turbulent change is because of communism's complete failure as an economic system to improve living standards or to compete in this technological age.

Enhancing economic strength is the priority of the world's nations now more than ever. Accordingly, certain priorities need to be recognized and acted upon if our country is to enter the next century as a world leader. We need to anticipate and prepare for an acceleration of current trends, which will separate economic winners and losers.

Emphasizing education is absolutely essential. The increasingly interdependent world economy is a service-and-information one, based upon technological innovation and understanding. Where is there a place for the uneducated in technologically intensive businesses? Without extensive education, today's children will be tomorrow's unemployed or part of the developing "underclass" of never employed. The generally sorry state of public education must be reversed by a commitment to a "War for Education." Corpus Christi's Athena Program is an excellent example of quality public education.

Entrepreneurial abilities and traditions in America have been the world's best. Maintaining this edge will require adaptability in order to change rapidly. The better-educated will be more adaptable to the exciting changes taking place and the pace of change may only be expected to escalate.

Ethical decision-making will be an integral part of the economically strong's agenda, as will the power of inspiring ideas. Democratic ideals have not been equaled as motivators for mankind. Ask, "Is it right and will it be beneficial to those concerned?"

Ending the erosion of our international competitive position also requires political changes. One recent former Japanese Prime Minister resigned to accept responsibility for the "loss of confidence in politics among the general public." Alienation from government and those governing might be turned around if U.S. politicians accepted this level of accountability. As an example, we have two houses of Congress that recently voted themselves a pay raise. They may feel that they deserved a reward because they have not bankrupted the U.S. Treasury yet; they have only turned us into a large debtor nation. High ethical standards have been exhibited by those congressman and senators who would not stand for re-election because they did not achieve the goals they sought, including the balanced budgets to which their constituents and the American public are entitled. They are today's true patriots. Hundreds more should follow their example.

Elect officeholders with the vision, the capability and the guts to lead. Terms in office should be limited by time or by achievement, not by how long before someone has to be carried out or thrown out.

Ensuring a focus on the importance of America's economic strength will require more than an eye-catching presentation. Eventually, economic realities will determine our power as a nation and the character of future life for our children and ourselves.

Do We Need A Constitutional Convention?

(Published June 28, 1997)

It has been 210 years since the Constitutional Convention of 1787. It established the structure of our federal government and the way it operates. Suppose a Second Convention was organized this year, and you were elected a delegate. What priority changes would you propose?

This challenging issue was put to American Rhodes Scholars - including two recently selected from Corpus Christi, Mary Meaney and Ana Unruh - in their quarterly publication *The American Oxonian.* Other Rhodes Scholars may actually be involved in shaping answers to these questions, including President Clinton, Supreme Court Justice David Souter and more than a dozen current U.S. senators and members of Congress. For all of us, considering such questions may be challenging.

At the outset, we should all remember that the U.S. Constitution has been amended only 27 times, including the Bill of Rights, which is the first 10 amendments. The enduring strength of the greatest nation in the history of the world indicates that constitutional change should proceed cautiously. Nonetheless, whether by amendment or other corrective action, a number of issues merit attention.

One of my principal priorities would include electing members of the U.S. House for a three- or four-year term to reduce continuous campaigning and fundraising. Addressing campaign-finance reform would be one related priority. With the federal government granting communication licenses, some fixed amount of free or inexpensive airtime should be an important component of reform.

Some of our country's great achievements come from courageous risk-taking and from elected leaders acting out of principle and conviction. More effective solutions to problems may be anticipated by reforming campaign financing. Public officials may be relied upon more to exercise independent judgment if they are less beholden to special financial interests upon whom they must rely under the current system.

Due process and rights of those accused under our criminal laws have been constitutionally protected throughout our history. Modern times have created a need to balance the rights of innocent victims of crimes more equitably.

Another change would be to fix an automatic termination date for appropriation legislation, i.e., sunset laws of three or five years. This would require the federal government to do zero-based budgeting. Our priorities need to change from not only trying to balance an annual budget, but to also address the re-payment of $5 trillion of debt.

Is it time to revisit the allocation of seats in the U.S. Senate? Why should Texas and Rhode Island have the same number of senators? There are 19 states with 38 senators, which have a total population less than California. Smaller states, perhaps, should have one, and larger states, perhaps three senators.

Mandating term limits has been an objective for some who believe that change would improve the effectiveness of the Congress. My view is that we have a mechanism for limiting terms. It is called free elections.

Discussing, considering, debating, and addressing such questions has historically been how this wonderful country has continued to improve, and become even better. Irrespective of your answer and point of view, thinking about these issues and those like them is vital to the health of our democracy.

Rule Of Law, As Well As The President, Is On Trial

(Published January 16, 1999)

"The rule of law is essential, whether it is preserving, or seeking to create, a free, democratic society. One of Russia's most difficult challenges is to effect such a rule of law." So spoke Lady Margaret Thatcher at the 1998 Spohn Lyceum in Corpus Christi.

Reflecting on the importance of respect for the law seems especially timely as the impeachment trial of President Clinton unfolds. The implications and consequences of these proceedings are far-reaching. One aspect of the process merits special focus: the efforts of some participants to influence the outcome by pro-active public relations, rather than relying exclusively on the legal process mandated by the Constitution.

The trial must be - and must be perceived as such - fair and consistent with our highest principles of justice. It would be unfortunate if the ultimate vote of the senators (jurors) was along party lines; each of the 100 senators has taken an individual special oath to uphold the law as a juror. Chief Justice Rehnquist and the Senate have a special responsibility to reaffirm our rule of law - dispassionately and fairly.

In the past, certain high profile trials have generated considerable publicity. Nonetheless, most Americans accept the information and misinformation communicated by external forces as informative, but not dispositive of specific allegations. Results are expected to be consistent with the facts of the case and not a consequence of peripheral activities. This standard has been gradually eroding to where we now have concerted efforts to let public opinion determine the outcome of judicial procedures. The Clinton impeachment trial crystallizes the issue. Should polls, popular opinion, public relations, "spin doctors," and similar phenomena play any role in determining the outcome of legal proceedings? Should decisions be reached exclusively through even-handed, impartial processes based upon directly relevant evidence?

If the former prevails, what happens when a businessman, whose company's products are widely admired, a popular movie or sports icon, or a scientist with a record of great discoveries is accused of a crime? What happens when someone is innocent of a crime, but whose behavior is condemnable? Should their fates depend upon external factors, such as popularity or political posturing, or should a dispassionate judicial process be determinative?

Whether President Clinton receives high approval ratings, or whether we live in peaceful, economically robust times, is not the relevant issue at hand. We are at a place where both our rule of law as well as the president are on trial.

Whether President Clinton is guilty of perjury and obstruction of justice, or not, or whether such crimes constitute conduct requiring removal from office, or not, must be decided by the Senate based upon what is presented in the trial only; that is the standard which will have legitimacy. Otherwise, we undermine respect for the law by differentiating those who have the ability to influence public opinion from those who do not before the law.

Thomas Jefferson's words in his first inaugural address are as compelling today as they were then:

"Equal and exact justice to all people, of whatever state or persuasion, religious or political...The wisdom of our sages and the blood of our heroes have been devoted to their attainment."

Section VI

United States Political And Related Issues

A Mixture Of History And Irony

(Published September 29, 1984)

The words placed it in perspective: "In the history of this country, tonight is only the seventh time that a dinner has been held in Statuary Hall in the U.S. Capitol. The first time, Lafayette was honored by the Congress for his contribution in winning the Revolutionary War. The last time was when Queen Elizabeth was honored during the Bicentennial celebration. Tonight, we honor former vice president, almost president Hubert Humphrey." So began a tribute to Humphrey in Washington a few weeks ago. As one looked around that famous hall, each state had contributed the sculpture of one of its heroes; Sam Houston represents Texas.

The Humphrey family invited 150 people for the dinner, the award of a Congressional Gold Medal presented by President Reagan the next day, and for the dedication of a sculpture in the Senate. These events were outstanding - and filled with history and irony.

The White House and the Humphrey family tried to schedule these tributes at a time and in a manner that would be as nonpolitical as possible; mid-September of 1984 was selected. The speakers did not discuss the current political campaign, yet they included Humphrey's fellow Minnesotan, Walter Mondale, and Republican Sen. Dole; they were among those who praised Humphrey and who were his good friends.

Perhaps most ironic was that the most moving speaker in honoring Hubert Humphrey was Ronald Reagan. Early in the careers of each, they had been mutually supportive. Mr. Reagan endorsed Humphrey when the latter first ran for the U.S. Senate in 1948. Mr. Reagan and Humphrey later diverged on many issues. Nonetheless, President Reagan was very positive in his tribute. He especially noted former Vice President Humphrey's strong anti-Communist views. Both Mr. Reagan and Humphrey believed in dealing with the Soviet Union from a position of strength.

As we were leaving the White House ceremony, several historical observations relevant to today were discussed among the guests.

Since Humphrey narrowly lost the 1968 election, the country has wanted stability and continuity in the presidency; this is due, in part, to the chain of events initiated by the man who defeated Humphrey by a few hundred thousand votes. Many people now would like to see a president serve two terms, which has not happened since the 1950's. Would Humphrey's loss of the presidency to Nixon now contribute indirectly to President Reagan's re-election?

Some tried to speculate whether Mondale could close the gap in the short time until the election as Humphrey had done 16 years ago, and go even further to win. Perhaps the factor most difficult for Mondale to overcome is the strength and momentum of the economy. Underlying the economic success, ironically, are large federal deficits. Nevertheless, the results of elections have shown that people tend to vote their present sense of economic well being.

Those attending included Democrats, Republicans and independents. It may have been one of the few times between Labor Day and election day this year that some of these people will be in the same room and not debate each other. It was reassuring, however, to know that, for a brief time in a heated campaign, politics could be put aside and a committed and compassionate American could be appropriately honored. It also reaffirmed the irony of history.

Vice President Hubert H. Humphrey
AP/WIDE WORLD PHOTOS.

How Much Truth Can A Candidate Tell, And Get Elected?

(Published January 9, 1988)

Some time ago, a friend and I obtained the motion picture rights for the next novel of William Styron, whose previous book, "The Confessions of Nat Turner," won a Pulitzer Prize.

We were told by virtually every expert that Styron's new book was too powerful and penetrating to become a feature film; it portrayed reality with too much poignancy. Nonetheless, our production company made "Sophie's Choice" and Meryl Streep received the Academy Award for best actress for her portrayal of Sophie.

The issue of how much reality the American public truly wants is very timely. As we enter 1988, the most important mission facing this country is to decide who will lead the nation into the last decade before the 21st century.

The political pundits and experts caution the current candidates for president of the United States against addressing the issues realistically and completely. Too many vested interest groups could be offended. They say that a candidate who acknowledges that taxes need to be raised along with effecting spending cuts cannot win. Former Vice President Mondale's experience in the last presidential election is remembered on this point. Nonetheless, I believe that the American electorate is adapting and changing; voters should respond to that candidate of either party who asks the hard questions and provides realistic and intelligent analyses and answers.

From 1945 until 1973's oil embargo, our American economic power underwrote peace, prosperity and relative predictability in much of the world. Our relative position has steadily eroded since then, and has deteriorated markedly recently. The candidate with the courage to say that our consumption and debt binges must end, that we cannot continue to borrow and debase the dollar, and that strong measures must be taken for a period of time, is the one we need. So far, most of the current candidates are finding subterfuge in jargon like "revenue enhancement," or are avoiding difficult issues in some comparable pussyfooting manner. With the intense interest in the "character" of the candidates, it will be important to know who will tell the truth about what policies are necessary, including painful ones; many believe that "the truth does not win elections."

Leadership of the kind, and with the character, that built this country should find the American people responsive; that means someone not primarily motivated by power, prestige, or place in history. Someone tough, creative, capable, and forthrightly truthful should be electable this year; the job, the challenges, and the times require those qualities.

We are not anointing a saint. Facing reality may require acknowledging that some of our greatest leaders were human, had weaknesses along with great strengths, and still advanced the national interest and the will of its people. Perhaps this is the year to test those specific aspects of "character" that are most relevant. Wouldn't the majority of American's vote for someone who committed to specified policies and programs, to assist in reforming the way the Congress functions, and to not seek re-election unless certain goals were accomplished?

It seems appropriate to conclude with the insightful words of a literary friend of William Styron's, James Baldwin, in his "The Fire Next Time."

"Celebrate what is constant - birth, struggle, and death . . . and apprehend the nature of change, be able and willing to change. I speak of change not on the surface, but in the depths - change in the sense of renewal. But renewal becomes impossible if one supposes things to be constant that are not - safety, for example, or money, or power. One clings then to chimeras, by which one can only be betrayed, and the entire hope, the entire possibility of freedom disappears."

Meryl Streep
AP/WIDE WORLD PHOTOS.

In A Toss-Up Election, Texas Will Play A Pivotal Role

(Published August 6, 1988)

Without a crystal ball and a guarantee that it works, it is challenging to foresee what may happen in a national election with so many moving parts. Nonetheless, it is difficult to resist making some observations about this year's choices, having been a member of the national campaign staffs of presidential candidates in two prior elections.

George Bush will be the first incumbent vice president since Hubert Humphrey in 1968 to officially be his party's nominee for president. Bush will soon face Humphrey's dilemma - being loyal to the president, or putting forth his own ideas and qualities of leadership. As did Humphrey, he is starting far behind in the polls. A key to this election will be how quickly Bush gets organized and projects his positive vision for America and his personal ability to lead the country. It took Humphrey too long; while he caught up to within one percentage point, it wasn't enough.

There is no burning single issue like the Vietnam War was in 1968. We can expect to hear less about specific programs and more about personal capability, experience, and accomplishments, or lack of same. Far more than recent elections with major substantive differences, this will be a test of character and competence under pressure.

This election should continue the trend of crossover voting, with many people not making up their minds until close to Election Day. The depth of commitment to either party's ticket will probably be shallow. While some of our fellow citizens have viewpoints that accommodate no shades of gray and are passionate in their party commitments, a large number of people have discovered the limits of ideology. They recognize that both parties sound like the other at the center. The wings of both parties represented by Jesse Jackson and Russell Long, and Lowell Weicker and Jesse Helms, respectively, are currently relatively muted. Both parties echo the other on many issues.

Which party wants economic development, a decrease in the deficit, more opportunity for all Americans, focus on family and community values, increased attention to education, and a continuing relaxation of tension with the Soviet Union? You guessed correctly: they both do. The Democratic Party will seek to project itself as the party of fiscal responsibility - best equipped to deal with the deficit. The Republican Party will argue that it is the party of opportunity - best equipped to sustain a strong economy and spread the benefits to more of our citizens. This campaign should be full of paradox and humor - and, ironically, some truth.

History may provide some perspective on this election. Like 1960, the Democratic candidates are currently elected officials from Massachusetts and Texas. The Texan is a well-respected senator and a brilliant choice. The Republican candidate was an incumbent vice president. The 1968 election is relevant as described above. The 1976 election is instructive because it is the last time a Democratic governor with no national experience ran for the presidency with a senator as his running mate. The Republican candidate in that year was solid, but not perceived as bold.

Some other interesting points about the three elections described above are that neither party had a candidate who was an incumbent president who had been elected to that position; all were close elections. Each represented the end of an era, and the beginning of a new one - and so it will be in this election no matter who will be our next president.

George Bush and Michael Dukakis share more similarities than differences. Both grew up on the East Coast and have had extensive careers in public service. Both reached their current positions against long odds over time; both are cautious and persistent. Further, both are pragmatic. How else could Dukakis have selected Lloyd Bentsen and Bush be an advocate of what he once called "voodoo economics?"

When the debating, marketing, one-line sloganeering and campaign humor are over, our next president will be the person best able to communicate a vision of our national future that emphasizes basic values, extends the promise of opportunity to more of our citizens, and seeks to restore our international competitive position. His message will be positive.

Finally, candidates of both parties have a home base in Texas, and it will accordingly be vital to both parties. No Democrat has been elected president since Texas became a state in 1845 without its electoral votes. For the next three months, my unclear crystal ball shows only one certainty. The classic "the eyes of Texas are upon you" will be transposed to "the eyes of the country are upon Texas."

Texas Should Keep An Eye On New Jersey Governor's Race

(Published August 19, 1989)

Women, their rights, and their issues have been advancing in our generation. From art to zoology, women contribute and often excel. In government, Margaret Thatcher remains England's powerful leader and catalyst of change. Benazir Bhutto guides Pakistan. In Japan, a historical first was achieved this month when two women were appointed to the cabinet after women's issues precipitated a change of control in the Diet.

In this country, only last week at the U.S. Military Academy, a woman was appointed as the first captain on the Corps of Cadets - which made history at West Point.

It is against this background and positive trend that I remember a conversation at a reunion last summer with a college classmate, Jim Courter, a congressman from New Jersey. He is deeply interested in the issues facing the nation and his state and has plans to address them.

Courter is his party's candidate for governor of New Jersey. His opponent is also a multi-term congressman. When elected early in November, the new governor will be the only official elected statewide in one of the few bastions of real political power in this country. Under New Jersey law, the governor appoints the other state officials, including the members of the judiciary and the attorney general. New Jersey thus has two candidates each of whom has addressed major issues for more than a decade who will have considerable authority and ability to implement programs when elected. However, their respective views on vital matters such as education, the environment, economic development, crime and drug issues are no longer the focal points of the campaign.

Beginning early last month, when the Supreme Court announced its Webster decision, an unexpected issue emerged which could dominate New Jersey's gubernatorial election and could determine its outcome: the issue is women's rights. It contrasts a woman's individual right to have an abortion with governmental regulation or limitation of that choice. Specifically, it is whether the nation's law on the subject, as expressed in the landmark Roe v. Wade decision, as restricted in the Webster case, will be changed - either nationally by the Supreme Court in future cases, or the Congress - or on a state-by-state basis. While Webster sustains a woman's right to choose an abortion, it may be a selective right depending upon her financial circumstance and in which state she chooses to exercise her right.

The question of individual choice, or governmental regulation of that choice - so-called pro-choice versus pro-life respectively - is potentially one of the most difficult and divisive issues facing our country. The debate on the issue is reminiscent of similar debates 20 years ago about Vietnam. Both sides are very emotional and passionate: bitterness and hostility punctuate most discussions. As some feelings ran deep about Vietnam due to ideology, some accordingly run deep on this issue due to theology. People don't necessarily speak rationally with each other. They often speak with mass demonstrations and occasional violence. While the issue is clearly important, it appears even more so because of the fervor of communication.

Instead of addressing the many public issues facing a large state, it currently appears as through this women's issue may play a prominent role in New Jersey's upcoming election - out of proportion to the totality of public concerns. The candidates are currently being required to address the subject to the exclusion or minimization of other serious problem areas.

The risk for us is that what is presently happening in New Jersey could be a microcosm of what could happen in other states, or nationally. An issue such as this could continue to be so emotional and pervasive as to divide the nation. It would obscure other pressing needs, and be a diversion from the resolution of other very important public concerns. While we become pre-occupied, other nations can obtain competitive advantages in various areas which we would neglect. It threatens to have a negative impact for years; this issue could become the Vietnam of the 1990s.

Accordingly, what finally happens this November in New Jersey is of consequence for us. If the women's rights issue remains primary and pervasive, it would be an unfortunate irony and potential national tragedy in an otherwise positive world and national trend regarding women, their rights, and the issues that affect them.

Will '92 Shape Up As A Landmark, Troubled Year, Like 1968?

(Published January 11, 1992)

The year 1968 was a landmark year and turning point in American political history.

It began a virtual lock on the White House by the Republican Party, which proceeded to win five of six presidential elections. Respected analyst Kevin Phillips accurately foretold this at the time. Recently, both in his book, "The Politics of Rich and Poor," and in public statements, Phillips predicts a national rejection of Republican economics and politics. Although political power has been divided between the parties in the executive and legislative branches, the voting public has held the president more accountable than it does the Congress. Will the presidency change this year? Will Phillips be proven correct again?

That year, 1968, was also the year which shaped my view of the dynamics of presidential elections. I was asked to join the national campaign staff of then-Vice President Hubert Humphrey, who was preparing for his role as part of President Johnson's re-election effort.

On March 28, 1968, President Johnson surprisingly announced that he would not seek re-election. We then became part of Humphrey's presidential campaign organization. Although my first responsibility was coordinating a comparison of the candidate's positions on the issues, I soon developed a keen appreciation for "the swift and dramatic change factor" in national politics, which often transcends, and even supersedes, the issues. The ability to respond is often determinative.

There are obviously major differences between 1968 and 1992. The times and forces are different. In 1968, both parties' candidates were nationally known; in 1992, this does not appear to be the situation. Nonetheless, it may provide a useful perspective to consider certain parallels between 1968 and the present to see if 1992 could be a threshold year.

The times were turbulent and unsettling in 1968 as they are today. While such conditions would seem to favor the experienced and known candidate, uncertain times produce unpredictable voters.

As the assassinations of Martin Luther King, Jr. and Sen. Robert Kennedy, the disorderly National Democratic Convention, and the frustrating Vietnam War experience were unanticipated events which shaped 1968, so might we expect surprises this year. The presidential election of 1992 will likely be decided by an event or events, which have yet to occur. While foresight is always difficult, it is especially so in troubled times such as those now being experienced both domestically and internationally.

There was a buoyant stock market in 1968 as there is now; however, serious and fundamental economic problems existed then as they do currently.

The Vietnam War was the mega-issue of 1968, as the state of the economy appears to be this year's major issue. The actual difference on the issue between Nixon and Humphrey was marginal; what was significant was how they were positioned during the campaign. Similar blurring of image and reality may be expected this year as both parties have politics determine policy as they try to outbid each other with stimulative economic proposals and blame each other for our problems.

President Bush is being challenged in the primaries by two opponents, as Humphrey faced McCarthy and Robert Kennedy in 1968. The political similarities are noteworthy as the incumbent party is again divided over direction. The respective extreme wings and demanding special interest groups contend that the centrist candidate has betrayed the party's principles.

The intra-party challenges were harmful to Humphrey, and may be expected to hurt Bush. While Humphrey did recover, and was rebounding from a stormy convention, he was unable to overcome those problems in time. The election was close, and may be expected to be so this year.

The "vice-presidential variable" was significant in 1968 with both Humphrey and Nixon having held that office. Another aspect of the "vice-presidential variable" will likely be very important this year with confidence in Vice President Quayle likely to be critical to the election's outcome.

A further parallel is that we entered 1968 with the conventional wisdom such that the incumbent party in the Oval office was expected to be re-elected despite Vietnam. We enter 1992 with a general expectation that President Bush will be re-elected despite a multitude of domestic problems. Events overtook and shaped reality in 1968, and may be expected to in 1992.

Accordingly, the election result in 1968 was less a vote on the issue or issues, as it was the consequence of diverse forces coming together on a given day. Momentum was going Humphrey's way after a seesaw year; he lost by half a percentage point. Many people felt that one more week would have changed history. In such unsettled times, especially with today's instant communications, this can be the reality of politics irrespective of polls, positions on some issues, and predictions.

The certainty about 1992 is that it will be an eventful year with rapid and dramatic changes. As citizens we shall need to monitor developments, analyze our alternatives, and vote. We shall not know until the ballots are counted on Nov. 3 whether 1992 is a landmark year, as was 1968, and whether Kevin Phillips will be two for two.

Perot's Candidacy Has Been A Delight And A Disappointment

(Published October 24, 1992)

The winner of the 1992 election can be announced today: The American people want to vote for change. No presidential candidate has received the depth of support as has the public's expression of the desire for effective change.

The inability of the federal government to address significant problems, the runaway deficit, and the failure to adjust priorities in a rapidly shifting world are some of the reasons that account for this protest against the status quo.

Each candidate now claims to be the candidate of change. Perot promises fundamental change in a one-term administration. Clinton promises new policies and new people in a new administration. In the past few weeks, even President Bush is promising new policies and new people in his next administration.

The two-party gridlock in Washington is one of the primary causes of this momentum for change. No one has expressed the public's frustration better than Ross Perot has. Arguably, the two most memorable statements of this year's campaign were made by him on the subject, i.e., "I don't have any experience in running up a $4 trillion debt. I don't have any experience in gridlock government." The other inferred that an extra-terrestrial must be responsible for our problems because both Republicans and Democrats deny responsibility.

But Ross Perot's candidacy has been a simultaneous highlight and disappointment. Two questions were asked of a close associate of his by this writer a number of months ago. The answers were prophetic and provide a valuable perspective, not only on Perot, but also on President Bush, Gov. Clinton, and the election itself. The questions were, "Is Ross Perot qualified to be president?" and, "Can he be elected, and do we want him to be?"

The first answer was that Perot has significant strengths and weaknesses, different in their specifics, but comparable to the other candidates. "If one of the major party candidates had fewer liabilities and greater proven capabilities, Ross wouldn't be running. If this year's choices included someone truly outstanding, as we have had at previous times in our history when he was needed, Ross wouldn't be doing this."

Secondly, he observed that, "this level of the political arena is unfamiliar to Ross." Nonetheless, he thought he could win, "if the country is ready to face its problems and Ross decides that he is willing to go through the process of getting elected. If the voters want someone who is no politician, but is a citizen-patriot, action-oriented, and a practical problem-solver, we would want him there; he is not perfect - in that regard, he is like the other two."

With the election 10 days away, votes vacillate among the three choices. Each has exceptional abilities or he would not be a serious candidate for the nation's highest office. Nonetheless, each choice has significant positive and negative aspects. President Bush speaks of what he tried to do and how he would try harder. Gov. Clinton articulates promises of what he will do, and claims he can do. Ross Perot talks about what should be done. Bush has known weaknesses. Clinton is untested in national office. Neither has an unblemished record for candor or consistency on relevant subjects. Perot said that he is not political, and he has demonstrated it.

With change anticipated, why is the mood of the country so cynical? Perhaps it is because the public senses the gridlock between the two major parties is intransigent. The Republicans want to balance the budget by cutting government programs and reinvigorate the economy by cutting taxes. The Democrats want to balance the budget by raising taxes and to reinvigorate the economy by government spending. For a decade, the Democrats have permitted the Republicans to cut taxes without cutting spending and the Republicans have let the Democrats maintain spending programs without raising taxes to pay for them. Both have been irresponsible, and the result is our crushing deficit.

On a deeper level, however, this gridlock may reflect the ambivalence in the American public itself. We all support, in principle, programs for the poor, the elderly, health insurance, etc., but few of us have been willing to make the sacrifices, and vote for the increased taxes necessary to support these noble objectives. In this way, the ambivalence of the two parties reflects our own ambivalence.

A potential tragedy of this election is that the public's apparent willingness to vote for change suggests that it is ready to "face its problems." The public remains cynical because it questions whether either major party candidate will really provide the necessary leadership for change. The independent candidate who has addressed the issues most forcefully has the longest distance to travel to effect this message; however, it has been heard.

Nation Has Changed Utterly Since The Riotous Times In 1968

(Published August 28, 1993)

The 25th anniversary of the violence and protest at the 1968 Democratic National Convention in Chicago occurred earlier this month. That unrest was an important turning point in our nation's history. Some observations seem appropriate.

The turbulence was a significant factor in Hubert Humphrey's loss a few months later in one of America's closest presidential elections. Certain significant changes in the nature of presidential leadership, political courage, and the public's confidence in government and political involvement may be traced to that time.

Lyndon Johnson was president in 1968. His faults notwithstanding, he may be viewed in retrospect as our strongest president since FDR. He had the support of much of the country after President Kennedy's assassination. He knew and managed the Congress better than any president in this century. His landslide victory in 1964 provided a clear mandate for his exercise of power. He utilized that strength primarily on the twin issues of civil rights and Vietnam, and chose not to run again.

Johnson handpicked Humphrey as his vice president and potential successor. If the violence of August 1968 had not occurred, or the election had been a few days later, the history of the latter part of the 20th century might be very different.

As it happened, a generation has passed during which the very nature and meaning of leadership changed. While Humphrey is generally remembered for advocating certain domestic policy initiatives in a liberal tradition, he stood with the strongest of conservatives in defense of his country. In fact, he was among the few civilian leaders who risked his life for his principles as he survived machine-gun attempts on his life from the militant Communist Party in Minnesota.

Such leaders were pro-active, obtained legislative results, and resolved pressing problems. They were not afraid of the consequences of pursuing policies based on conviction and principles. They were prepared to fight unpopular battles for what they believed to be right and in the country's best interest.

In contrast, in recent years, some of our most talented leaders express themselves by resignation in frustration at their inability to make the federal government function effectively. U.S. Senate leaders like Howard Baker and Warren Rudman voluntarily left office because of their inability to be effective and responsive to our country's problems. More House members chose not to run for re-election in 1992 than at any previous time.

These resignations serve to highlight the problems, but they don't solve them. While we seek heroic leadership, the problems we face are complex and deep-rooted. A whole new generation of leaders may be required who not only have courage, vision, and ability, but are able to work together in the national interest for an extended period to effect meaningful change. Structural adjustments, like term limits and the expanded use of independent commissions, may be necessary prerequisites for a number of people working cooperatively to provide the leadership in order that America re-find its way.

Confidence in our political system began to erode in 1968 and accelerated with Watergate a few years later. One clear contrast between then and now is the way people respond to that which touches them the closest. There were vocal protests on national issues and a belief that government could and would solve those problems that were its clear responsibility. Today, people are far more cynical and disengaged. They question the effectiveness of the political system and almost all politicians. The declining number of Americans who register and vote each election is one indication of this growing cynicism.

For example, there is no organized pressure to address the epidemic of violence in our country, as we should - firmly and resolutely. More Americans were murdered in America since 1990 than died in Vietnam in a decade of war. How long can we read and listen to tragic news reports, accumulate statistics like this, and maintain our way of life.

The vantage point of a quarter of a century provides perspective. It doesn't assure answers. We may have to accept that we do not, or may not, have a giant of a leader to solve our problems. Nonetheless, we could move out of gridlock and apathy if people in positions of leadership followed the advice of Mark Twain to, "Do the right thing because it would please some people and astonish lots of others."

Can We Get Beyond The Superficial?

(Published October 5, 1996)

One month before a national election and one day before the first presidential debate is an appropriate time to consider what the taxpaying public receives for its funding of campaigns. Considerations of great issues should precede elections, but such discussions have become superficial and frequently limited to 30-second advertisements and short sound bites.

We need fewer flash details about episodes in candidates' lives and more facts regarding what they think about the real issues that affect us. As the public is now paying a significant amount of the cost to make presidential campaign financing more fair, is there an opportunity to raise the level of campaign content?

One of the many ways of guiding the content of presidential campaigns to a consistently higher level would be to require that some percentage of public funds be used to research and communicate positions on long-term, vital issues. For example, a host of foreign policy, national defense issues, alternative ways of approaching and financing socially responsible programs is insufficiently addressed. Rhetoric substitutes for thoughtful, problem-solving creativity. Let's consider how one aspect of one important issue might be reflected upon were changes in the content of our presidential election campaigns modified and mandated.

Few subjects are of greater consequence than those related to education. How is education going to have to change to prepare people to deal with constantly expanding knowledge? Throughout history, a central purpose of education has been to acquire a relatively fixed body of knowledge. A symbol of this outlook was Oxford University's library in the Radcliffe-Camera Building, which was circular with no room for expansion. In theory, one could learn all knowledge, which was finite.

As insights and ideas of the past shape many aspects of life and society today, our general approach to education is rested in a time before the Information/Computer Age. For some time now, knowledge has been expanding at a pace that can no longer be assimilated by any individual; the pace is accelerating. Acquiring the knowledge available in the world is an impossible concept. Information is being organized, used in research, and transmitted internationally in a way that will transcend boundaries and effect great change in the way the world and its people operate as we move into the next century.

What are the implications of unprecedented technological changes upon the nature of education? As so many aspects of society are in transition to the Information/Computer Age, how shall education change?

One option would be to change the emphasis from acquiring knowledge beyond an agreed-upon basic core curriculum to equipping people to think critically and independently. A focus on developing judgment and a discerning mind rather than memorizing aspects of knowledge that is ever-changing may better anticipate the requirements of the 21st century.

A question for the coming debates may be which of the candidates has developed a vision for America which promises to perpetuate our values in the dimensions of 21st century life. What would be the nature and goals for the education of tomorrow's emerging generation? Consideration of fundamental, important issues as a greater percentage of presidential election content would be a greater contribution to our national well being than much of our current communications. It is our country. It is our money. Why should not the quality be consistent with the cost and the importance to the American public?

Section VII

Personal Insights, Values & Character

Outward Bound Offers Insights

(Published October 17, 1981)

"I regard it as the foremost task of education to ensure the survival of these qualities: an enterprising curiosity, an undefeatable spirit, tenacity in pursuit, . . . and above all, compassion." - Kurt Hahn, founder of Outward Bound.

These words were read to the 20 of us who comprised one class at the North Carolina Outward Bound School a few weeks ago; we heard frequent passages each day as we completed another part of a most challenging course in a remote wilderness area. We were all participating with our host, who indicated that a similar Outward Bound program in another part of the country had substantially altered his life four years ago.

Outward Bound is a non-profit, educational organization that uses experiences in a wild, natural environment as a teaching medium.

Part of what occurred was like a trip out of James Dickey's *Deliverance* as 17 men and three women steered and paddled rafts over the rapids and waterfalls of the Chattooga River. Among many other undertakings, we lowered ourselves by a rope from the top of Pickens Nose Mountain to a rocky ledge 100 feet below while looking down thousands of feet over a precipice. We exchanged all that was familiar and comfortable in our daily lives for an experience at a level of essentials, an adventure with the unfamiliar that was far more than a course in survival. Many of us spend considerable time reliving the past or anticipating the future; Outward Bound helps focus upon the present moment!

The purposes of Outward Bound include encouraging people to confront seemingly difficult tasks by calling upon unrecognized reserves and strengths. It further emphasizes a sensitivity to nature, a recognition of significant responsibility to others in your group and a commitment to service in your community.

The repetitive patterns and habits which go unexamined for long periods are tested when we leave the safety of home, family, friends, and routine for such an experience. This excellent program provided a time to examine one's value structure and personal priorities, implications and possibilities. Many of us think about basic, important matters only when confronted by personal tragedy and loss, or when stunned by an unexpected event. Perhaps the most demanding challenge and unknown that we faced in the mountains, on the rivers, and in the wilderness was our time of complete solitude and reflection.

While in that North Carolina wilderness, I decided to conclude this column on this page of commentary with one of the more poignant quotations that was read:

"It's not the critic who counts. Not the man who points out where the strong man stumbled or where the doer of great deeds could have done better.

"The credit belongs to the man who is actually in the arena . . .

"And, who, while daring greatly, spends himself in a worthy cause so that his place may never be among those cold and timid souls who have known neither victory nor defeat." - Theodore Roosevelt.

'Mindpower' Vital Resource

(Published October 9, 1982)

"We go out because it is in our nature to go out, to climb mountains, and to sail the seas, to fly the planets and plunge into the depths of the oceans . . .. We extend our horizon, we expand our being." - W. Noyce

On this last day of National Higher Education Week, it seems appropriate to consider the thought above and to make a few observations about the idea that "America's energy is mind power." This theme has been discussed around the country this week, including at Del Mar College and Corpus Christi State University.

In view of our current economic problems, which will lead to difficult choices of resource allocation, the importance of higher education needs to be emphasized. It involves a long-term commitment to our best asset - our people. It is an investment in those who will contribute to society in the future. We want to develop capable minds to be better citizens, to continue to unravel mysteries of life, and to understand ourselves and our world.

On an individual level, generations of Americans have progressed through intelligence and higher education; success has been achieved in this country more through education and knowledge than origin or social rank; the latter were determinative in most other countries throughout history. While there are gifted or very lucky exceptions, higher education has provided the primary vehicle for significant mobility and opportunity. Because one of the few certainties in life is the presence of risk, there is a continuing quest for meaningful choices. Those who choose to acquire skills and knowledge applicable to an information-oriented, high technology age will enhance their opportunity for achievement.

Two further observations may be made. First, higher education should be a public policy priority for many reasons. Totalitarian countries place a disproportionate amount of resources into education; while, in part, it is a vehicle for indoctrination for them, it is also a resource in competition with us and others in the free world. Not only in space exploration, medicine, and other fields, but in national defense, "mind power" is the critical variable;

look at the results of superior technology recently both in the Falklands and in the Middle East where Israeli American-built planes destroyed 80 Syrian Soviet-built planes without a loss. Until genuine peace exists, strong minds lead to stronger countries on every level.

Secondly, academia has increasingly produced actual leaders in addition to advisors. It has provided a growing number of people who formulate and implement domestic and foreign policy. For example, American foreign policy for more than a decade has been orchestrated by a succession of men with clear roots in higher education and advanced knowledge - Kissinger, Brzezinski, Haig, and Shultz, the current secretary of State. As a graduate student in the mid-1960's, I remember participating in a course that featured lectures by two young professors - Kissinger and Brzezinski. However you may judge the results of their services, the fact remains that a succession of presidents with different political philosophies have turned to individuals with roots in institutions of higher learning to help them develop and execute America's foreign policy in these perplexing and challenging times.

When we look at the world today, we see the fateful consequences of yesterday's lost opportunities. As priorities are now determined, higher education should be recognized as an opportunity and encouraged in order to continue to "extend our personal horizon and to expand our national well-being."

A New Generation Commences To Cultivate The Garden

(Published June 3, 1989)

What could be more important during this time of year than commencement exercises and convocations? While not often front-page news, the advancing of a new generation is history in the making. On the occasion itself, one or more of their own, or a guest speaks to assembled graduates, honor students, and their relatives and friends. We may recall the best of those speeches that we have heard - and think of what we might say were we to address such a group of young people today.

One remembered address referred to the story of a mythical village called Thracia. It was the custom for young men and women to climb a nearby mountain on graduation day. At the summit, each would see a vision of the viewer's future. They would descend and spend their lives fulfilling that predetermined destiny. The point of the story is that soon after graduation, real life frequently begins with its limitless possibilities and uncertainties. While some may wish for absolute answers as provided on the Thracian Mountain, what is truly significant is how you conduct yourself on your own life's journey, which will only become known as you live it.

Another memorable commencement message communicated several ideas. It recalled the harsh world outside academia and reminded graduates of their responsibilities to family, friends, community, and country. Each generation faces the challenges of its time - war, ignorance, prejudice, drugs, crime, high unemployment or whatever. All present were encouraged to be part of the solution to the problems of their age, to be compassionate, to strive for excellence, and to be swayed always by beauty and truth. Self-development was emphasized; strive to become a person with recognized capabilities and clear convictions. Do your best with whatever abilities you have; as Voltaire said, "Cultivate your garden." Retain your ideals and memories while being pragmatic and adapting to contemporary realities. The speaker didn't say that life would be continuously simple and easy!

Were we to speak at a commencement exercise today, we might incorporate some of the above, and suggest some other thoughts.

One thought is to take risks and be tenacious in pursuing goals; do not fear failure or ridicule. Thomas Edison is said to have failed in almost 9,000 experiments before "discovering" a long-lasting light bulb filament. When asked about dealing with so many failures, he is reported to have replied, "Failures? Nonsense. I'd say 9,000 successes. I've learned about 9,000 formulas that don't work."

While taking chances, try to make your dreams a reality. One of life's tragedies is that not enough people fulfill their dreams.

Differentiate between dreams and illusions, and pursue your dreams. Aristotle observed over 2,500 years ago that young people "have . . . not yet been humbled by life or learned its necessary limitations; moreover, their hopeful disposition makes them think themselves equal to great things." Dream great things and do your best to accomplish what you can.

A corollary of pursuing your dreams is to not count on a second chance to lead your life a certain way. A movie currently being exhibited, "Field of Dreams," is a mystical, wishful story that provides a mechanism to re-live certain times and experiences. Real life rarely offers such an opportunity; try to live it as you want the first time.

Finally, enjoy life consistent with your vision of what is important. Try not to merely pass time, but take action in whatever direction is appropriate for you. You need not be quite as adventurous as Indiana Jones in another currently popular film about his Last Crusade. Nonetheless, if you can combine adventure with humor as well as he does with his feature film father, you will attain high achievement - and have fun.

"In the time of your life, live - so that in this wondrous time you shall not add to the misery and sorrow of the world - but shall smile at the infinite delight and mystery of it." - William Saroyan.

Spring Is A Good Time To Examine The Priorities In Your Life

(Published May 23, 1992)

Spring is a wonderful and beautiful time of the year. It is the season of awakening, rebirth, and constructive change. Flowers bloom, spirits soar, and each day seems to offer limitless possibilities. It is a time of sensitivity to nature - and to ourselves.

A few weeks ago, a friend suggested conducting an interesting experiment. It can be done anytime, but is especially encouraged during this season. It is not recommended to anyone who is not prepared for challenging self-scrutiny, nor to anyone incapable of change.

He wrote a list of that which he valued most in his life; he considered thoughtfully and carefully what he valued and what was most important to him. The list included his relationship with those whom he loved the most - his children, spouse, other family members, and close friends; it included his health and physical condition, career goals, economic success, his religious faith, his intellectual objectives and search for answers to life's questions, etc. He then ranked these in approximate priority order.

For the next week, he kept a record, divided into half-hour segments, on how he spent his time. At the end of that first week, he added up the hours and compared them with his priorities.

The results were so surprising and startling that he was convinced that he had experienced an "atypical week." He kept the list for a longer time period, but the conclusions were virtually the same. What he learned was that there was a major discrepancy between what he said was important and how, in fact, he spent his time, channeled his energies and attention, and conducted his life. One person who took this "test" now schedules two hours in the middle of the day three times a week to work out at a health club.

This season of rejuvenation may be an appropriate time for each of us to think about the relationship of our values and priorities to the actual ways that we lead our lives. If we care about our community, region and nation, shouldn't we re-allocate personal time and resources to express and advance those convictions? Can we continue our patterns of pursuing isolated individual, cultural, and economic interests while the quality of life in our society suffers and atrophies? We must fulfill our civic and patriotic responsibilities as generations before us have done, as required by the circumstances of their time. We must address the issues of the approaching 21st century.

On a personal level, if our values include a passion for a person, a belief, a place, or a sunset, we may need to rediscover that and make it part of our lives now. "Where have the years gone?" How many of us ask that question when only memories can be found? How we dread the time that we shall call or go to see that special person, that parent, and learn that they won't be there - again.

We know to what and to whom we have deep commitments, although we may not always act accordingly. We like humor and adventure, but may not have enough of either. We may enjoy listening to country music and dreaming, but don't. We like to read, but think about it more than we do it. We don't ever read or re-read inspiring works like Kipling's "If" or Cavafy's "Ithaca," which offer great insight into life and ourselves.

Understanding the realities and the dimensions of the lives that we lead offers the option of constructive change. Self-appraisal may not provide all the answers, but it can lead to a more fulfilling personal pilgrimage and the knowledge that we are trying to spend our time and energies in a manner consistent with that which we feel and believe.

"Look to this day,
For it is life, the very life of life.
In its brief course lie all the
verities and realities of your existence;
the bliss of growth, the glory of action,
the splendor of beauty.
For yesterday is but a dream and
tomorrow is only a vision,
but today well-lived makes
every yesterday a dream of happiness
and every tomorrow a vision of hope."

- The SUFI, 1200 B.C. (from the Sanskrit)

Americans Must Find Strategies For Dealing With Change

(Published February 27, 1993)

"Change" is the most descriptive and often-used term of our time. It has become as certain as death and taxes and affects us on many levels.

It seems appropriate to reflect upon a few aspects of "change." This is fitting because of the era in which we live, when dramatic change alters the world. Our country recently voted for change and is now considering what specifically that means on a potential scale not seen since President Lyndon Johnson's Great Society almost a generation ago. It includes my personal heightened awareness of change. If for no other reason, it is appropriate to reflect on change because the first day of spring is exactly three weeks from today; it is both the season and symbol of change.

Change is a powerful and complex word - powerful enough to shape lives, elections, and destinies, and complex enough to require considerable space to define it in Webster's Third New International Dictionary. While President Clinton exhorts us to "make change our friend," effecting personal change is no easier than implementing societal or cultural change.

We are frequently ambivalent when making or facing change. We are attracted to change as an idea. However, while we seek a new direction, we also want to retain that which is familiar and comfortable. Change challenges tradition and our sense of continuity. We are truly often happier with what once was, or might have been, rather than with adjusting to what is, or could be with certain changes.

Further, regarding personal change, insightful writers about women and men, such as in "Passages" and "The Seven States of Man," respectively, describe changes that we all inevitably experience. How many of us accept these facts, or, even more, prepare for them? While many changes have considerable elements of predictability, we are surprised when the expected becomes reality.

The ability to prepare for change is vital on many levels. For example, successful investing combines judgments on the direction of the economy, interest rates, industry trends, and other factors; in short, it requires the ability to anticipate change and act upon it.

While lessons learned through our experiences help us respond to change in our careers and the world around us, we are often not fully prepared to handle or adjust to change in our personal lives and the world within us. There is a need to increase consciousness about understanding, accepting, integrating, and then moving forward with the personal changes that we face, whether through loss, growth, or "triumph or disaster."

With change a necessary part of life, how much specific education do we receive regarding it in our schools, our colleges, or in adult education? While it is implicit in our studies and important to our lives, it is neither expressly taught nor consciously addressed except when we are required to deal with it. How often is the subject addressed among close friends or within a family? It is easier to ask, "What's on TV?"

Most available insights come from professionals or counseling groups that come into play after a crisis and when a person is in need of help. Why does such vital learning have to begin after damage is done?

Some indications that change merits study and understanding as a subject of distinct focus are emerging. A new field of evolutionary medicine is developing. The recent "Odyssey of the Mind" elementary and middle school program in Corpus Christi included reading about the concept of change.

The reading could have included these words of Reinhold Niebuhr, “God, give us grace to accept with serenity the things that cannot be changed, courage to change the things which should be changed, and the wisdom to distinguish the one from the other."

New Standard Of Responsible Citizenship Is Emerging

(Published May 1, 1993)

A radio station recently played a hit song from the 1960s, "Turn, Turn, Turn." The lyrics were inspired by the Bible (Ecclesiastes 3:1-8): "For everything there is a reason and a time for every purpose under heaven: A time to be born, and a time to die." Listening to it recalled my college and graduate school days. Those memories provided some thoughts about 1993.

Like today, the early 1960's were a time when a "new generation of Americans" assumed the highest offices in our nation's capital. A young, vigorous, and controversial Democratic president was elected without receiving a majority of the popular vote. The vice president was a former U.S. senator from the South. The president claimed that he appointed "the best and brightest." Questions were asked about his competence, character, and popularity. His only daughter's first name began with C. His wife received considerable media attention and publicity. The seasons do "turn" - and return.

Certain teachers offered insight then about the cyclical nature of prevailing values in our country as well as political phenomena. Our culture and politics shift from authoritative to permissive, from more individual freedom to more sense of responsibility. Human nature seeks what it does not have as our culture mirrors our lives - up, down, always seeking equilibrium while rarely achieving it.

Cultural values proceed in a direction until excesses create reactions the other way, and then the process repeats itself. Periods of self-indulgence and unbridled ambition are followed by times of community sensitivity and responsibility. For example, the socially conscious 1960s followed the more traditional and predictable 1950s in our country. In reaction, the 1970s and '80s witnessed an increasing emphasis on materialistic and achievement-oriented standards. The beginning of the end of that era was symbolized by the story of the largest business takeover in financial history, which was told in the best-selling book and recent Home Box Office movie, "Barbarians at the Gate."

This emerging value shift can be found on a number of levels. Nationally, President Clinton has proposed a new national service program to put young people to work helping implement solutions to some of our nation's pressing social problems in return for college tuition benefits. Motivating factors are comparable to those which led President Kennedy to create the Peace Corps in the early 1960s. An aspect of the plan is to emphasize the importance of voluntary action so that greater numbers of people will honor their responsibility of citizenship.

South Texas is in the forefront of this emerging standard of citizenship responsibility and volunteer action. Caring for, and about, others is an integral part of life for many people in this area. In fact, the extent of the spirit of volunteerism here is part of the attractiveness of living in this part of the country. Within the past few weeks alone, we have learned of the generous actions of retired senior volunteers, helped children, obtained three replicas of Columbus' ships from Spain, walked to benefit the March of Dimes, cleaned beaches, held Buccaneer Days, contributed to the world's hungry and to the search for a cure for cancer, and recognized the *Caller-Times* Jefferson Volunteer Award recipients. Other life-enhancers received Sharing Time and Resources Awards sponsored by the Volunteer Center of the Coastal Bend.

Many people, of course, act according to these values continuously, irrespective of prevailing cultural and/or political imprimatur. Outstanding examples of significant contributors are among us; they have been here for a long time irrespective of cultural cycles and public recognition. As these caring values are shared more broadly and deeply, our community, society, and country benefit. Hopefully, the heightened social consciousness of the 1990s will lead more people to use their personal, financial, artistic, athletic, or other abilities for some worthy cause and higher purpose.

Perhaps, when these prevailing cultural values reach their cyclical "turning" point, as history has taught us to expect, we may actually have begun to truly address a number of our problem areas. We may have citizen volunteers who are really making a difference in "turning" around our country. This offers the greatest and most tangible promise that we shall get satisfactory results. For instance, if enough people held public office for a limited time who were motivated only by public service, not politics or re-election, we might really deal with issues. We could then assure the preservation of the best of our way of life for much longer than foreseeable on our present course.

In the meanwhile, let's contribute as we can to standards of responsibility, service, and a re-emphasis of family bonds and other enduring values. Let's consider the words of Stephen Grellet:

"I expect to pass through this world but once. Any good thing, therefore that I can do or any kindness I can show to any fellow human being, let me do now. Let me not defer nor neglect it; for I shall not pass this way again."

Great Lessons For The Endless Unfolding Of Life's Challenges

(Published December 18, 1993)

This is a special time. The end of one year is approaching, as is the beginning of another; we are moving closer to a new century. The holiday season is one of celebration, remembrance, and personal perspective.

It seems appropriate to pull back from the constant stream of news, issues, and information that we regularly digest and to consider that which is of greatest importance - our life, our character, and our spirituality.

One way of obtaining perspective is to read outstanding writings and then think about their wisdom and insight. Whether religious or secular, powerful and moving books and other written works can provide inspiration for personal reflection and renewal.

There is no perspective clearer than thinking about one's purpose on this relatively short journey between life and death.

At this time, I would like to share some of my favorites with you. Perhaps one of them will cause you to reflect on events of this past year with greater insight. Perhaps one of them will assist in dealing with next year's challenges and opportunities.

On the journey of life, C.P. Cavafy wrote eloquently when he said:

"When you start on your journey to Ithaca.
pray that the road is long,
full of adventure, full of knowledge . . .
that the summer mornings are many,
that you will enter ports seen for the first time, . . .
Always keep Ithaca fixed in your mind.
To arrive there is your ultimate goal
But do not hurry the voyage at all . . .
Ithaca has given you the beautiful voyage.

Without her you would never have taken the road . . .
With the wisdom you have gained, so much is precious,
you must surely have understood by then what Ithaca means."

On the strength of character required to perpetuate our uniquely American democracy and ensure freedom for future generations, Ralph Waldo Emerson said that we need:

"Men and women of original perception and original action who can open their eyes wider than to a nationality . . . men of elastic, men of moral mind, who can live in this moment and take a step forward."

On character and on sound priorities and values, Rudyard Kipling's classic words merit their immortality:

"If you can keep your head when all about you
Are losing theirs and blaming it on you, . . .
If you can dream and not make dreams your master . . .
If you can meet with Triumph and Disaster
And treat those two imposters just the same;
. . . If you can make one heap of all your winnings
And risk it on one turn of pitch-and-toss,
And lose, and start again at your beginnings
And never breathe a word about your loss;
. . . If you can fill the unforgiving minute
With sixty seconds' worth of distance run,
Yours is the Earth and everything that's in it
And - which is more - you'll be a Man, my son!"

On respecting that which is eternal and transcends our daily interests, a great Indian chief named Seattle said:

"The president in Washington sends word that he wishes to buy our land. But how can you buy or sell the sky? The land? The idea is strange to us. If we do not own the freshness of the air and the sparkle of the water, how can you buy them? . . .

"The water's murmur is the voice of my father's father . . . earth is our mother."

Alfred, Lord Tennyson, best articulated values of commitment and re-dedication when he said:

"Tho' much is taken, much abides; and tho'
We are not now that strength which in old days
moved earth and heaven, that which we are, we are. -
One equal temper of heroic hearts,
Made weak by time and fate, but strong in will
To strive, to seek, to find, and not to yield."

Finally, John Gardner, author of "Self-Renewal," spoke directly to us a few years ago in a commencement address when he said:

"Learn all your life. Learn from your failures, from your successes, learn by taking risks, by suffering, by enjoying, by loving, by bearing life's indignities with dignity...

Your identity is what you've committed yourself to. If you make no commitments, you're an unfinished person. Freedom and obligation, liberty and duty, that's the deal. There are men and women who make the world better - by the gift of kindness or courage or loyalty or integrity. It really matters very little whether they are behind the wheel of a truck, or running a business, or bringing up a family. They teach by living it.

Life is an endless unfolding, and if we wish it to be, an endless process of self-discovery, an endless and unpredictable dialogue between our own potentialities for learning, wondering, understanding, loving and aspiring . . . life's challenges . . . and the challenges keep coming. And the challenges keep changing."

Best Role Models Are Sometimes The Nearest

(Published January 28, 1995)

When I was growing up, young people often found heroes worthy of that accolade among public figures. Some of my heroes included presidents of the United States, military leaders from World War II and Korea, athletes, and entertainment personalities.

How the world has changed! Today, becoming a public figure is virtually an invitation to intense investigation and potential denigration. Rapidly rising stars in politics, athletics, entertainment, and business often soar - only to fall quickly with embarrassment. Indeed, if my presidential heroes were in the White House now, I wonder how heroic they would be under today's scrutiny.

Nonetheless, young people and all of us need heroes and role models. I believe they still can be found where they have always been - closer to home, within our family, circle of friends, and our community. Many real heroes are more private, quiet role models than heralded public figures. Nonetheless, they merit celebration, respect, and emulation. For my family and me, my father was such a private hero. We recently marked the fifth anniversary of his death. His was a life well lived on his own terms.

My father was an ordinary person with extraordinary character. He believed in the classical virtues. He was independent and happy with his life and never judged or envied others. He was a warm, caring person whose values were mainstream and solid - consistent with his Midwestern upbringing. I do not ever remember hearing him complain as he relished the wonder of life; he felt that each day was a gift. He most enjoyed that which was simple and basic - family, love, close friends.

He was a gentle and soft-spoken person. I am told that he was his most aggressive as a starting guard for his high school football team in Indiana. One could only learn of his athletic success from others. The only hint that he provided was his lifelong commitment to physical fitness - stopping only when cancer's progression made exercise impossible - which included his dancing; he loved music and dancing.

He taught his children and grandchildren mainly by example although his rare advice was incisive and memorable. "Do your best with your abilities."

To each family member, he would say, "Always take care of each other and those in need."

My father was self-reliant, supportive, flexible, and very funny; he had a great sense of humor. He also had a deep interest in well-expressed insights into life, some examples include:

"We shall not cease from exploration and the end of all our exploring will be to arrive where we started and know the place for the first time."
- T.S. Elliot

"Eternity is not something that begins after you are dead. It is going on all the time."
- Charlotte Gilman

"It is never too late to be what you might have been."
- George Eliot

"Your children's souls dwell in the house of tomorrow, which you cannot visit . . . For life goes not backward nor tarries with yesterday. You are the bows from which your children as living arrows are set forth."
- Kahlil Gibran

He had an irrepressibly positive view of life that was shared by my mother. "Life is too short for petty people or concerns. At the end of life, few people wished that they had spent more time worrying, criticizing, or being negative. Don't lose perspective about what really matters."

We live in an era when public heroes rarely retain their luster. Perhaps this will not be so significant if we look closer to home for our heroes; we shall honor and remember them forever.

Harry Klein

Entrepreneurs Are Living The American Dream

(Published April 20, 1996)

The Great Age of Entrepreneurship is one description of our time that will almost certainly be applied by future historians.

Whether it is the expanding global dimension to opportunity, advancing technology and communication, strong equity public markets, significant restructuring and change, or a combination of these factors, interest and activity in entrepreneurship have increased tremendously.

The American Dream remains very attainable as people are inspired by leading entrepreneurs like Warren Buffett, Dan Lufkin, Wayne Huizenga, Jay Pritzker, and Bill Gates.

The 1995-96 academic year is approaching an end and with it my appointment as adjunct professor of business at Texas A & M University-Corpus Christi. The students in my Seminar on Entrepreneurship have a real interest in the subject consistent with the national trends. I learned from the members of my class, and, hopefully, taught them as well.

We viewed entrepreneurship both as an approach to business and as a philosophy for life in our time. The basic principles of entrepreneurship can be applied either to start a new business or to revitalize an established one. The entrepreneurial philosophy can further enhance one's life well beyond material success; it is a way to conduct much of one's entire life.

The main elements of classic entrepreneurship include identifying an opportunity, organizing resources and committing, and being willing to take certain risks to proceed amidst uncertainty to achieve a worthwhile objective. Perhaps, the most important element is to focus upon key factors for success and persevere irrespective of difficult challenge and adversity. Of course, certain personal qualities are necessary - competence, concentration, high threshold for hard work, confidence, daring, and motivation derived from solid values and worthwhile purposes.

As more people with demonstrated entrepreneurial talent apply themselves to public service, the possibilities for major contributions to our country and its communities are extraordinary. The creativity required for problem solving, the personal standards, and the results orientation of successful entrepreneurs offer the ability to make a very meaningful impact on society.

People who become real doers are inspired in many different ways - by a spiritual or secular experience, by inner needs, by an example worthy of admiration, or by a powerful and moving idea that is heard or read.

Each of the students shared a favorite inspirational reading with our class; they demonstrate my confidence in the potential and the values of this emerging generation, which should contribute positively to the Great Age of Entrepreneurship. Following are some of their selections:

"Always bear in mind that your own resolution to succeed is more important than any other one thing."
- Abraham Lincoln.

"You gain strength, courage, and confidence by every experience in which you really stop to look fear in the face . . . you must do the thing which you think you cannot do."

- Eleanor Roosevelt.

"A human being should be able to change a diaper, plan an invasion . . comfort the dying . . . program a computer . . . cook a tasty meal . . . die gallantly. Specialization is for insects."

- Robert A. Heinlein.

"The ache of unfilled dreams is the worst pain of all."

- Anonymous.

Take Time To Admire The Art And Grandeur Of Nature

(Published June 15, 1996)

The nation's largest grassroots environmental organization, the Sierra Club, recently elected a 23-year old new president; he was actively supported by his 83-year-old predecessor.

What a clear, factual and symbolic expression that the younger generation wants unpolluted air, water, and land!

The young executive intends to engage his contemporaries to join others to advance wilderness preservation and respect for the natural world and its ecosystems as top priorities for our country.

This is good news for all of us.

Often, when nature or the environment makes news, it is bad news, i.e., extreme heat or cold, tornadoes, etc.

The fact that we are in the hurricane season and that an extraordinary drought is battering parts of the country, including the Coastal Bend, is consistently in the news.

It is important to remain aware and vigilant regarding the destructive potential of nature. Accordingly, our consciousness and respect for its power and role in our lives can often be perceived negatively.

In fact, experiencing and enjoying the natural beauty and wonders of the world are among life's greatest pleasures and treasures of memory. Whether your favorites are sunrises or sunsets over the Gulf of Mexico, the Laguna Madre, or the Aransas National Wildlife Refuge in South Texas, or the Grand Teton Mountain Range in Wyoming, or the fjords in Norway, or wherever, the beauty and majesty of nature is frequently unheralded in our time.

As we approach the next century, the pace of life, fascination with evanescent celebrities, epidemic marketing, and technology/computer/internet obsessiveness prevent many people from appreciating the unique simplicity and grandeur of nature.

As Thoreau said, "Heaven is under our feet as well as over our heads."

In addition to providing visual pleasure, focusing upon nature can reteach or reaffirm many of life's most important lessons.

One is to learn to adapt and change to survive and thrive amidst fast moving, shifting conditions.

Another is to recognize that matters of immediate concern can be placed in proportion to the universe and eternity and, accordingly, be seen in proper perspective, thereby becoming less important and stressful.

We can reflect upon the continuum of life of which we are all a part. Only the most intense of people will dwell on their problems when viewing or thinking about the ocean floors, tall mountains, or far away galaxies and solar systems.

One of this century's best-known young persons was forced to spend much of her life restricted to an attic. She speaks for many with her eloquent expressions of her feelings. "Go outside . . . somewhere quiet along with the heavens, nature, and God. Because only then does one feel all is as it should be and that God wishes to see people happy, amidst the simple beauty of nature. As long as this exists, and it certainly always will, I know that then there will always be comfort for every sorrow, whatever the circumstances may be." Anne Frank, "The Diary of Anne Frank."

What's The Secret Of Success?

(Published November 23, 1996)

Thanksgiving traditionally begins the year-end holiday period, which is so special for many of us.

It is a traditional time for being with family and friends whom we love, for remembering those who are no longer with us, for being especially helpful to those less fortunate, and for reflecting on our lives and how we lead them.

It may also be a time when young people may be receptive to constructive advice.

One of the most valuable suggestions that I heard many years ago is to be, and remain, positive in your life.

Dr. Norman Vincent Peale described the thought well in his "The Power of Positive Thinking." This power encourages one to focus on opportunities rather than dwell on difficulties. "The optimist sees the doughnut while the pessimist sees the hole."

The consequences of not thinking positively, and missing opportunities accordingly can be significant.

One prospective investor looked at the Ford Motor Company and concluded, "the horse is here to stay but the automobile is only a novelty - a fad."

A former movie executive considered the script for "Gone with the Wind" and concluded that, "No Civil War picture ever made a nickel."

While a certain caution and common sense are often appropriate, some of the greater lost opportunities and unfulfilled dreams come from actions not attempted, rather than risks of efforts that were taken.

This quality of being positive and advancing in life has been essential for both individual success and national achievement in America.

Theodore Roosevelt admired a person "who, while doing greatly, spends himself in a worthy cause so that his place may not be among those cold and timid souls who know neither victory nor defeat."

Ralph Waldo Emerson believed that much of America's extraordinary success was due to people "who can live in the moment and take a step forward."

President Kennedy reinforced the point: "Let us go forth to lead the land we love, asking His blessing and His help, but knowing that here on earth, God's work must truly be our own."

Viewed over the long term, history reflects an inexorable trend of progress - almost generation after generation.

Those who have participated in the growth, development, and forward momentum of their time have had a higher return on their lives than others have.

Those who "do" rather than "not do" with their lives may make more mistakes, but they will also climb more mountains, see more sunsets, take more trips, laugh more, and probably experience far more of life's memorable passions.

Being positively inclined is a re-affirmation of faith in life and the ability to cope with adversity when encountered. It is an attitude to be applied to the day-to-date obstacles in life while discovering one's full potential.

The ever-changing environment at the end of the 20th century creates continuing challenges and opportunities in many aspects of life.

Desire, determination, vision, combined with a positive, pro-active orientation can lead to exceptional results - and even - more enjoyable future holidays and memorable times.

Dr. Norman Vincent Peale (author)
AP/WIDE WORLD PHOTOS.

You Have To Risk Failure To Succeed

(Published April 5, 1997)

After a recent class, one student asked a very tough question. "Is it worth the hurt to take a significant risk, be vulnerable, and then not succeed?"

History and life reward the risk-takers. Those who are unable to risk failure are less likely to become independent, fully capable individuals or great achievers.

Those who can handle occasional setbacks are far more likely to succeed. They will not collapse when faced with major challenges, criticism, or even rejection. In fact, they often view them as a necessary part of a learning process and integral to developing powerful personal determination. They see all experiences as opportunities, including problems and difficulties.

Those who push their personal limits, seek to discover their unique potential, and try for that which may be unattainable will have more opportunities to be successful and find unrecognized strengths as they persevere. Those who experience reversal and do not maintain their desire to succeed will be defeated in the matter at hand, and, more importantly, in their attitude toward life itself.

It is a challenge to explain to those who have not faced major adversity or suffered traumatic experiences in their lives in a way that they will really understand. The emotional pain from setbacks often obscures their importance in building character and confidence; these usually precede genuine success and the development of inner strength.

The person running for public office, trying to be an entrepreneur, seeking membership in a private organization, or whatever-at-risk effort, may not succeed in that endeavor, nonetheless, he or she improves the probability of being the very best that he or she is truly capable of being.

This applies to the student who chooses more difficult subjects and thereby expands his or her personal limits and growth potential.

Those who strive for excellence or "stretch" objectives are likely to experience disappointment. However, they are more likely to become or do that which is truly outstanding. At least one top tennis player said that if he did not hit the ball out at least 10 percent of the time, he was not trying for enough winners to become a truly great champion.

Individuals with character and compassion will have empathy and try to make the lows not unbearably low for those who try and "are actually in the arena." Thoughtful, real people and fellow venturists will offer comfort and encouragement; in truth, they know that they could be in your place. The ferris wheel of life continuously moves up and down.

Had I remembered the following at the time, my answer to that tough question would have included this quote by Theodore Roosevelt:

"The credit belongs to the one who is actually in the arena . . . who strives valiantly, who errs and comes up short again. And who, while daring greatly, spends himself in a worthy cause so that his place may not be among those cold or timid souls who know neither victory nor defeat."

Never Forget The Value Of True Friendship

(Published November 22, 1997)

"I would like you to know how important our friendship has been, and I want to say goodbye in person."

These were the words of a close friend shortly before his passing a few weeks ago. His life and death were extraordinary. Those who knew him were inspired by his courage, style, and strong commitment to his family and friends, exemplified by these final actions and words.

A masterpiece of a tribute to him at a service in celebration of his life referred to his "accomplished life . . . of passion tempered by reason."

He contributed enormously to his community, state, and nation and to all that benefit from his many and continuing projects.

A gifted insight that he shared with his friends was, "everyone should learn before they die what they are running to, and from, and why."

It often takes a powerful occurrence to provide pause in our fast-paced lives to focus on what is of most consequence. In this age of overload of information and activity, it is easy to overlook and underappreciate the value of real friendship in our lives.

Accordingly, this column is dedicated to raising the importance of friendship to a higher level in the consciousness of all of us.

A relationship based upon affection, regard, bonding, or shared experiences and values leads to true friendship. Loyalty is at its essence, although flexibility is often required to respect uniqueness and individuality. Those who are rigidly judgmental present challenges to actual and potential friends.

The warmest friendships are often those with a long history. Friends provide a living contact with the past while continuing to enhance one's present journey through life - often with good humor. There is a special significance in the praise or criticism of those "who knew us when." However, we also need to not become so totally absorbed with old friends that we become insular and miss opportunities to form new friendships.

As with any significant relationship, friendship over time requires effort and sacrifice. Hands-on, strong personal friendships become very meaningful, especially in times of need - personal or professional. The support, trust, comfort, and advice are without equal.

Today, emerging generations may face unique challenges in developing and enjoying great personal friendships as in the past. The cutting-edge technologies of computers, the Internet, and others offer ease and speed of communication, but frequently encourage less personal and in depth contact. Connecting in cyberspace cannot be a substitute for in-person interaction.

Nonetheless, from ancient to modern times, the value of real friendship has been recognized and celebrated. As we approach Thanksgiving true friends should be considered among our blessings.

"What is a friend? A single soul dwelling in two bodies . . . Without friends, no one would choose to live, though he had all other goods." - Aristotle.

Extraordinary Mysteries Of The Universe Are Unfolding

(Published January 24, 1998)

These are extraordinary times of scientific, and potentially, personal discovery. In space, astronomers, physicists, and other scientists are continuing to advance our understanding of the cosmos and some of the forces that shaped Earth and ourselves.

Comprehending the universe with the discovery of other galaxies, quarks, and black holes, Big Bang and other phenomena enrich our lives by stirring our minds through learning and our imaginations through mental adventure. Few of us are directly affected in our daily living by this expanding understanding of the universe. However, the potential to have a very direct and significant effect upon us exists if we think about our lives and how we lead them with the perspective of the birth and death of stars and how we fit in the history and development of the universe.

As the search for truth about the universe unfolds, it may be appropriate to re-examine our assumptions scientifically and personally. For example, centuries ago people believed that Earth was flat or that Earth was the center of the universe. Copernicus and Galileo challenged those assumptions, but at the time many people resisted their conclusions. Current insightful research and theorizing suggest the evolutionary nature of truth in this quest for knowledge. We need to be open-minded and prepared to change.

A recent report suggests that the universe could be as old as 15 billion years and that the processes that have underpinned it could continue forever. Our lives acquire a different significance from this perspective. Each time we contemplate the universe and decipher more of its mysteries, we might consider what this means for each of us in our individual lives. Accordingly, fundamental questions about the meaning and purpose of life may be viewed differently.

If more people pause to reflect upon how we spend our time from this extraordinarily long perspective of time and distance, day-to-day negative actions and emotions, anger, prejudices, and other untoward behavior appear even more petty and insignificant and may decrease. What is important may be placed in this context; life and death issues can be more easily separated from the small and inconsequential with respect to our individual lives and that of the universe. Imagine more people taking day-to-day actions based upon consideration of the nature of the universe and our place in it; it would be a kinder and gentler place.

By absorbing this new information about the universe and reflecting upon it, a personal re-assessment can take place. Many people may think and act differently as their view of the world and their place in it evolves.

"You are a child of the universe, no less than the trees and the stars . . . And whether or not it is clear to you, the universe is unfolding as it should. Therefore, be at peace with God, whoever you conceive him to be, and whatever your labors and aspirations in the noisy confusion of life, keep peace with your soul."

- Max Ehrmann, "Desiderata"

Character Shows In How You Treat Your Friends

(Published April 11, 1998)

How we relate to our past in general and old friends in particular can provide perceptive insights into someone's character and values.

Loyalty toward, continuing interest in, and commitment to old friends is often difficult to balance with growth and change in one's life. Some people find little or no balance.

At one extreme, some associate exclusively with old friends and become somewhat limited and narrow; they remain cliquish and let few new people into their lives.

At the other extreme, some continually change friends in an opportunistic and shallow manner; they usually do not include old friends in their new life.

Many of those people who do not retain their old friends are unable to sustain permanent relationships based upon mutual respect and understanding. Some need to manipulate or control; others may not be well centered as individuals. Behavioral experts would likely find deep-seated issues of inadequacy or narcissism or both.

People with depth and character find a way for old and new friendships to co-exist harmoniously. These people can grow as individuals and still maintain life-long friendships. Such continuity usually makes the present more meaningful and fulfilling.

Recently, footnotes to extensive news reports of the activities of two of the world's leaders provided insight regarding their handling of old friendships and the importance thereof.

Pope John Paul II, formerly Karol Wojtyla, had a childhood friend, Jerzy Kluger, with whom he had no contact for 27 years due to the exceptional circumstances of World War II and its aftermath. When reunited, their old friendship transcended history and time. When he became pope in 1978, he granted his first formal papal audience to Kluger and his family.

Pope John Paul II never forgot where he came from - and who was there with him. The pope later entrusted his old friend to serve as an intermediary between the Vatican and Israel, which led to the Vatican's formal diplomatic recognition of Israel and other ties. Their friendship, which began early in this century, continues to this day as the century draws to a close.

The other world leader, President Clinton, has a history of dispatching old friends with whom he was once close and moving on to others. While we do not know all the circumstances, and, perhaps, appropriate reasons therefore, the patterns and the actions of abandoning friends while moving ahead personally, is troubling.

At the annual Gridiron Club Dinner in Washington, one barb highlighted this characteristic, "Harold Ickes warned me - Socks, beware of Bill's capers; when he no longer needs you, you'll read it in the papers."

This very personal and human attribute of retaining one's historical friends, irrespective of the position reached in life, can separate truly great and outstanding people from those who are merely successful and popular.

"Life can only be understood backwards, but it must be lived forwards."

- Soren Kierkegaard.

Pope John Paul II
AP/WIDE WORLD PHOTOS.

Focus On Genuinely Transcendent Concerns

(Published June 20, 1998)

"So many people walk around with a meaningless life. They seem half-asleep, even when they are busy doing things they think are important . . . they're chasing the wrong things. The way you get meaning into your life is to devote yourself to loving others, devote yourself to your community around you, and devote yourself to creating something that gives you purpose and meaning . . . The important questions have to do with love, responsibility, spirituality, awareness."

These excerpts are from a book, "Tuesdays with Morrie," by Mitch Albom, which was recently given to me by a friend in Corpus Christi. It is the story of a student and teacher and offers a moving and insightful perspective on life and death for all of us.

Any time is a good time to slow down, think about our lives, and act out of a consciousness and awareness of what and who are truly important to us. Both Father's Day and the official start of summer will be celebrated tomorrow. Perhaps the coincidence of both will recall traditions of remembering and honoring parents and of memories of vacations and quiet times. They provide an opportunity for a change in one's priorities and approach to life as well as a change of pace.

We live in an era of overload, to-do lists, and clutter. With stressful, conflicting demands on our time, we are frequently running as though we are on a constantly moving treadmill. There is always too much to do and insufficient time.

Many of us become overwhelmed by work, goals, tasks, or whatever and push aside vital and meaningful human activities and relationships. We take loving relationships for granted. They need immediate attention, not continual postponements.

The essential lesson is to savor and appreciate the moment and not rush through life. If there are friends and family members that you have not seen for a while, take the time soon to be with the people who matter to you and genuinely care about you. Listen to the elders who want to share their individual experiences, stories, and wisdom. Tomorrow's tomorrow may not come. Distinguish what is deep, lasting, and eternal from that which is fleeting and temporal. The latter is of little consequence in the fullness of life.

Time and people pass far too quickly. Truly live in the present and fill your memory bank. Tomorrow can be all the more wonderful if part of today is spent in a way, and with those people, which and who truly matter. You will have the warmest of times and later remembrances of those who are no longer with you.

The essence of the lesson of "Tuesdays with Morrie" and of this season was summarized a few weeks ago in a masterpiece of a graduation address by a valedictorian of an area high school:

"Never be too wise, too busy, or too high-tech to remember what truly matters. What truly matters is to approach our lives with confidence, intelligence, curiosity, and caring."

Loyalty Was More Important Than The Presidency

(Published October 3, 1998)

When asked which three personal qualities are most admired, at least one thoughtful person responds, "Loyalty, loyalty, loyalty."

Loyalty is defined as being devoted to one's government, to one's obligations and principles, or to any person so deserving. Few subjects inspire the intensity of emotion and passion as those concerned with loyalty, or actual or perceived disloyalty. The implications and consequences are far-reaching on many levels.

One of my most vivid recollections of a significant issue of loyalty in operation occurred 30 years ago. For someone interested in public service at the time, it certainly changed my life.

I was a member of then Vice President Hubert F. Humphrey's national presidential campaign staff. For part of the year, I worked and shared an office with Stuart Eizenstat, currently Under Secretary of State for Economic, Business, and Agricultural Affairs. Our responsibility was to monitor and contrast the policy positions of the other candidates for president of the United States.

President Lyndon B. Johnson was unpopular in 1968, primarily due to Vietnam; this was a key factor in his decision not to run for re-election. The country was very divided.

Humphrey remained loyal to Johnson personally and was similarly committed to his policies. The Chicago riots and other factors notwithstanding, Humphrey's loyalty to Johnson was the major reason for his loss to Richard Nixon in what turned out to be a very close election.

One can only speculate on how different history might have been had Hubert Humphrey been elected president. While I was disappointed in the result, I nevertheless respected his loyalty both to President Johnson and to principle; this was consistent with his behavior throughout his career. He successfully led the fight early for a strong stand on civil rights (in 1948), advocated increased aid for education and medical help for the needy, and originated the idea for what became the Peace Corps.

This example highlights the prominence of the many issues of loyalty at top levels in the nation. The issue is an important one underlying present concerns in Washington. How will today's leaders resolve conflicting loyalties to people, to country, to personal beliefs and ambitions, and to our system of law and justice?

Beyond the public arena, issues of loyalty are relevant in all of our lives - in business, academic, interpersonal relationships - almost everywhere. Conflicting loyalties are frequently the most challenging of problems. As an example, if you are loyal to someone and that person violates a deeply-held principle of yours, what do you do? In a conflict situation between two people each deserving of your loyalty, what do you do?

Sometimes, a person who strongly believes in loyalty will face almost impossible choices. Raising our consciousness and discussing the subject may provide helpful insight.

Standards of loyalty, along with truth, honor, and other great values, are among the most important legacies passed from one generation to the next.

"It is not book learning young men need, nor instruction about this or that, but a stiffening of the vertebrae which will cause them to be loyal to a trust, to act promptly, concentrate their energies, do a thing - carry a message to Garcia."

- "A Message to Garcia," Elbert Hubbard.

Humphrey and Johnson
AP/WIDE WORLD PHOTOS.

Our Top Priority Is To Build Character

(Published June 5, 1999)

According to an ancient oriental proverb, if you plan for one year, grow rice, and for 10 years, grow trees. If however, you plan for 100 years or more, develop the capabilities and character of young women and men. When we recall that it was essentially the character of successive generations of Americans who created this great country, an action taken a few weeks ago is noteworthy.

Largely in response to growing anxiety over school violence, the U.S. Senate approved the creation of a national Commission on Character Development. If enacted into law, the commission would have two years to study "the impact of cultural influences on developing and instilling key aspects of character, which include trustworthiness, integrity, an ability to keep promises, loyalty, responsibility and a caring nature and good citizenship."

Proposing such a commission is in itself a significant statement about our times. Historically, values and character were shaped primarily by one's parents, teachers, friends and spiritual and religious beliefs. High standards of character and good citizenship evolved without formal studies by government commissions. Influences were fewer and more controllable then.

Isn't it ironic that as our country has progressed economically, technologically and scientifically to extraordinary heights, we feel the need to address character issues? Despite these advancements, we feel that traditional cultural values, such as those subscribed to by Tom Brokaw's "Greatest Generation," are at risk. That generation's exceptional achievements, sense of duty, modesty and understatement are less common today.

The causes of the current cultural turbulence, and the solutions, are complex. Legislation, private initiative, and a combination of both appear to be required.

Our commercially motivated culture has found financial success in promoting the excessively violent, profane and outrageous. Empathy for others is diminished by constant violence and sensationalism. The sacrifices of past patriots and the strength of our nation must produce something far more than a well-fed and well-housed audience for Howard Stern and Jerry Springer. Will so-called celebrities continue to supplant genuine heroes as role models for young people? Surely, we are destined for higher purposes.

Obtaining a solution consistent with our pluralistic society and our respect for diversity and individual expression will not be easy. A dilemma is inherent in trying to regulate content in a society rooted in free speech and free markets. Nonetheless, some focused efforts seem appropriate.

A need exists to re-emphasize the vital role of family. Increasing the time and attention that parents spend with their children is most important. While the vast majority of young people are terrific and developing well, some of their contemporaries need help and guidance through the many choices available.

Consistent with our country's tradition, individuals and groups have already taken some responsive actions. Gen. Colin Powell is chairman of "America's Promise: The Alliance of Youth" which is committed to mobilizing resources to help young people become good, productive citizens. The Horatio Alger Association of Distinguished Americans both helps young people facing specials challenges obtain a college education and conducts an annual study on "The State of Our Nation's Youth."

We have no greater priority as we plan for the 21st century.

Tom Brokaw
AP/WIDE WORLD PHOTOS.

Looking At The Past As We Approach Millennium

(Published November 7, 1998)

The upcoming year-end holiday season will be memorable. In addition to being a favorite time of year, this will be the last January 1st of the 1900's. While purists will officially recognize the next century and next millennium as beginning in 2001, most of us will celebrate something special in less than 14 months as we enter 2000.

Much of the discussion about the new century relates to computer issues, the so-called Y2K problem, or speculation on who will be elected the next president of the United States. While these and many other issues are important, the prospect of today's generations ushering in a new millennium is of such significance as to transcend other matters.

If one dates the recorded history of humanity to ancient Egypt in 4000 BC, this event has only occurred five times before. We have a unique opportunity to think about our lives in the context of time and history as we approach a new millennium.

In thinking where we are, and may be going, individually and as a society, it may be helpful to remember some of the previous pre-millennium and pre-century milestones.

One thousand years ago, the years 998-'9 were part of the Dark Ages with the Vikings of Scandinavia terrorizing much of Europe. The Holy Roman Empire was forming. The waterwheel, which later led to the creation of geared machinery, was introduced. The Toltecs ruled Mexico. One hundred years ago, William McKinley was president of the United States and Teddy Roosevelt's Rough Riders fought the Battle of San Juan Hill in Cuba during the Spanish-American War. Joseph Stalin began his political career in 1899 as a propagandist for railway workers.

One hundred years ago in South Texas, events were especially noteworthy and somewhat prophetic of the 20th century priorities. The first step to create a channel into Corpus Christi Bay was taken by Congressman Rudolph Kleberg;

he introduced legislation in 1899 that led to the initial dredging at Aransas Pass.

The first long distance telephone line arrived in Corpus Christi; it provided service only to Texas and Louisiana.

The military was already a visible part of Corpus Christi life as the city prepared to enter the 20th century. A company of Texas troops camped on North Beach, near where Zachary Taylor's men had been in 1845. A local militia, Kenedy Rifles, was organized to fight in the Spanish American War.

Thinking about our lives in relation to history offers an extraordinary opportunity for personal perspective. It provides a sense of belonging to something larger than ourselves. It heightens our awareness of the continuum of life and the passing of generation after generation. With such a view, we may develop greater insight into ourselves, the purposes of our lives, and what is truly important to us.

As we contemplate our own lives and mortality, we may dwell less on that which is insignificant in the larger picture. We and those who come after us will hopefully be most interested in concentrating our energies on learning the remaining secrets of the universe and of ourselves.

Good Judgment Is Critical In Information Age

(Published July 17, 1999)

A midsummer Saturday such as today is a time of rest and relaxation for most Americans. Across the country, whether on beaches, ranches, tennis courts, mountains, or in backyards, we are at leisure.

As we enjoy ourselves, we are also advancing the development of the most important personal quality for success in life – judgment. All experiences, whether at work or play, contribute to the development of individual judgment.

In this decade of rapid change before the 21st century, the exercise of sound judgment is as vital to a well-lived life as at any other point in history. Technology and telecommunications advances frequently alter our lives as information is aggregated and communicated with ever increasing volume and speed; how the information is used is what is truly important. Accordingly, good judgment must be applied to the marshalling of facts and the process of evaluating, discerning, comparing, and then arriving at a decision.

Those who do not utilize their judgment drift along and are carried by events or by the priorities and agendas of others. One college professor speaks of three kinds of people to demonstrate the consequences of not consciously making independent judgments; he refers to (1) those people who exercise judgment and make things happen, (2) those people who watch what happens, and (3) those who at the end of their lives say, "what happened?"

The use of judgment is required for decision-making in the conduct of our private lives as well as in public concerns.

Regarding personal matters, judgments regarding education, career, health, marriage, values, and goals are usually determinative of one's life and attendant happiness and fulfillment, or lack of same. Personal judgments are made continuously as alternative courses are evaluated throughout our lives.

With respect to public matters, had George W. Bush not reached the judgment that he could be elected governor of Texas in 1994 when a seemingly unbeatable incumbent, Ann Richards, was running for re-election, where would he be today compared with his current position and prospects?

In a number of situations, judgments about public issues impact private lives; they frequently differentiate the course of people's futures and fortunes. For example, with respect to economics and investments, those people who exercised the judgment that low interest rates, low inflation, globalization with its expanding markets, and the explosive growth of the information age would lead to increasing equity values participated in the extraordinary public securities markets of 1990's.

Many factors contribute to the exercise of good judgment; most important are the variety and nature of all life experiences and how they provide perspective for our judgment.

All experience is an arch wherethro' Gleams that untravell'd world of the future.

- Alfred Lord Tennyson, Ulysses

Governor George W. Bush
AP/WIDE WORLD PHOTOS.

World's Great Films Inspire and Motivate Us

(Published November 20, 1999)

As far back as I can remember, I have enjoyed and been entertained, engaged, and enlightened by movies. Accordingly, when the opportunity to attend the final three days of the Fort Lauderdale International Film Festival arose last week, I went to Florida.

The Fort Lauderdale film festival lasts longer than any other in the world - almost one month. More than 100 films from 30 countries were shown; films from England, France, Sweden, Greenland, Spain, Australia, Croatia and many other nations in addition to the United States were exhibited. Independent and foreign films as well as documentaries were presented.

One of the most moving films was *Windhorse* from Tibet. It is the first feature film shot in the Tibetan language. *Windhorse* shows the struggle for religious, cultural, and political freedom by the people of Tibet. Because of the repression in Tibet, the film was shot underground and many in the cast and crew were not identified for fear of retaliation against them or their families by the Chinese.

Film festivals are held, in part, to provide a forum for capable artists to communicate important stories, ideas, and public issues like *Windhorse* through movies, which may not be distributed otherwise. A veritable smorgasbord of cinematic art was available; it was cinema with something substantial to say. None of the movies were based on special effects or animation; they were about those subjects, which matter most to people at various stages of their lives.

Cinematic art, like other forms of art, speaks to the essence of our humanity. These films selectively and subjectively frame and arrange the world, communicating in a special way. The themes of these films ranged from powerful and wonderful to haunting and troubling, from intimacy to brutality, and from weakness to strength of character. Some portrayed life as comedy, even farce, while the viewpoint of others was serious drama, even tragedy.

Many of the films were about life and love. Some showed the resolutions of conflicts while others were more complicated and ambiguous; they required individual interpretations and choices, like life itself. Relationships among family and friends were focused upon as were the unpredictability of life and the inevitability of the need to cope and adapt to loss and change.

A concentrated three afternoons and evenings of these films led to some observations.

Most significant was the universality and commonality of human experience irrespective of ethnic or cultural diversity. Filmmakers in many different countries of the world explored the same subjects and had similar concerns and questions. Differences among people were transcended.

A deep reverence for nature was demonstrated in these films. The photography was beautiful and frequently awe-inspiring.

A recurring theme was respect for history and tradition and their role in shaping the present and future. Two movies especially portrayed this. One was *Postmen in the Mountains* from China; the other was *Baja California* from Mexico. The latter was about a man searching for inner peace and faith who returns to his ancestral home in the Sierra Mountains near the world's largest mural cave paintings; they had never previously been filmed.

In our hurried, competitive, and ever-more technological world, the role of art in our lives is especially important. Thoughtful cinematic art helps remind and motivate us to consider the universality of our human experience, and that which truly matters.

Section VIII

Outstanding Individuals

A Lesson From Twain For Today

(Published March 2, 1985)

"It is easy to find fault if one has that disposition. There was once a man who, not being able to find any fault with his coal, complained that there were too many prehistoric toads in it." – Mark Twain

1985 is an appropriate year to remember Mark Twain, the pen name of Samuel Langhorne Clemens, one of the most gifted writers in U.S. history. This year is the 150th anniversary of his birth and the 75th of his death.

One hundred years and two weeks ago today, his outstanding novel, "The Adventures of Huckleberry Finn," was first published in this country. "All modern American literature comes from . . . "Huckleberry Finn" . . . All American writing comes from that. There was nothing before. There has been nothing as good since," said Ernest Hemingway.

It has been some time since most of us read the story of Huck Finn's raft trip down the Mississippi River. We remember best the initiation into adulthood, the folklore of rural America, the possibilities of the frontier, and the affirmation of friendship reinforced by sharing great adventures. Mark Twain made insightful comments about human nature – both its light and dark sides.

He told his message with a sense of humor. "I am glad I did it, partly because it was well worth it, and chiefly because I shall never have to do it again." Mark Twain continued, "I was gratified to be able to answer promptly, and I did. I said I didn't know." His wit reinforced certain character values and national ideals.

Mark Twain's contribution to American literature remains a national treasure; they are a written legacy from a gifted person.

We need to encourage the development of gifted people today; they will grow to make contributions in many fields. As the Texas Legislature articulates its priorities in this important current term, let's not forget that talented people could emerge with little or no formal education during Mark Twain's relatively simple 19th century. As we approach the 21st century, however, in a far more complex world, we need to provide the public school infrastructure to facilitate the development of gifted children. All people continue to benefit from the accomplishments of the gifted in most aspects of our lives. Better prison conditions may be necessary, but not at the expense of developing the invaluable asset of the gifted new generation.

Mark Twain recognized the value of finding and developing gifted and talented people. In a tribute to such a person, he said, "Among the three or four million cradles now rocking in this land are some which this nation would preserve for ages as sacred things, if we could know which ones they are."

U.S. Produces The Best and Brightest, Like Ross Perot

(Published September 27, 1986)

During the month of September, most of us either begin a new school year, or recall those many Septembers past when we, too, were students. Attending, or thinking about school, tends to concentrate our thoughts either on the classroom or on some aspects of "the real world" to be entered. Earlier this week, an individual visited our city who personifies both a strong commitment to the quality of education in Texas as well as the best of what may be found in the real world.

Ross Perot is well known and admired not only as a successful businessman, as the person who played a pivotal role in reforming public education in Texas, and as a leader in the state's war on drugs. He is respected as an American patriot with deep compassion and commitment as described in the book and TV movie "On Wings of Eagles." His concern for his fellow workers led to his rescuing them from a prison in Iran. Underneath a quiet and unassuming manner, there is no question about his will or spirit. A number of observations come to mind, of which three seem worth communicating.

One is that our American educational system, and our broader national culture and atmosphere of freedom, produce far more of the world's truly great individuals and leaders than any other country. Japan's stratified, tradition-bound society may produce certain products less expensively. England's class structure may develop a certain number of very capable people. This country leads the world in producing creative, innovative, bold and outstanding individualists. The best and brightest of those make significant contributions to our way of life.

Secondly, we have some genuine heroes who can serve as excellent contemporary role models for younger people. The efforts of parents, religious leaders, writers, teachers, and others to instill values in students that help form good character are reinforced by visible, positive role models. Hype may create temporary celebrities; real heroes, however, act upon, and therefore symbolize, our most cherished values and beliefs. They forecast the future of the nation as examples of our youth. We identify with the feelings, aspirations, disappointments, and triumphs of those heroes and seek to emulate their standards.

Finally, no earthly power is greater than an unswerving commitment combined with a strong feeling. Our schools teach knowledge and develop skills, which are required to cope with, much less succeed in, this complex, fast-changing, and often confusing world. Along with other important parts of our culture, schools reinforce the need to combine knowledge with strong feelings to try to do the right thing for one's self, family, friends, community and country.

Even a brief exposure to Ross Perot and those other civilian and military heroes who are worthy of that description clearly shows that they share a fiercely passionate commitment to, and love for, doing their duty, and trying to do what is right - often at great personal risk.

"Some day after mastering the winds, the waves, the tide and gravity, we shall harness for Good the energies of love, and then for the second time in the history of the World, Man will have discovered fire."

-Tielhard de Chardin

Ross Perot (presidential candidate)
AP/WIDE WORLD PHOTOS.

'Red' Scott Knows Where To Find Life's Bottom Line

(Published December 13, 1986)

Occasionally, we have an experience, read, or hear something that has a deep impact on our lives. It is often unexpected and unanticipated.

Charles "Red" Scott, a native Texan and successful businessman, has the rare capability to have such an impact on other people - by his actions and his words. He is one of only 240 living recipients of the Horatio Alger Association of Distinguished Americans Award. Ten people annually are so recognized for having risen from humble backgrounds to prominence in different professions; their lives "must also typify strong community involvement and love of country." Horatio Alger Award recipients include Gov.-elect William Clements, President Ronald Reagan, entertainer Bob Hope, evangelist Billy Graham, coach Tom Landry, Supreme Court Justice Thurgood Marshall, golfer Chi Chi Rodriguez, singer Johnny Cash and retired Gen. Chuck Yeager. Former presidents Hoover and Eisenhower, as well as McDonald's founder Ray Kroc and air ace Eddie Rickenbacker, were members.

Red Scott was a featured speaker at a conference that I recently attended. Other speakers ranged from a top executive of Texas Air to a real-life Indiana Jones, a man who travels to and lives in the world's most remote places. Amidst these excellent speakers, Scott was nonetheless a standout with a talk entitled "Return on Life." All who heard him were deeply affected; it seems appropriate to summarize his words during this holiday season when we all seek togetherness with family and friends and personal perspective as this year ends and we approach 1987.

Most businesses and many people gauge where they are in their business or investments in terms of return on investment, or on equity, or on assets. Percentage returns are readily calculable and comparable. Red Scott's theme is that the most important return of all is a "return on life," and that most people don't take the time to think about it. He handed out four sheets of paper. The first was entitled, "These are the things I value the most." The second was, "Goals which I hope to achieve during my lifetime." Next was, "Things I would like to accomplish within the next five years."

Finally, "If I had only six months to live, here's how I would spend them."

On each page, under each heading, there were lines marked 1 through 20. Below were "to do" lines listed A through G. We were asked to list our responses under each topic, and then to enumerate specific tasks that would be required in order to realize those goals: the latter went on the "to do" lines. Scott requested that everyone answer spontaneously and quickly, and that answers not be shared with anyone. They were to be private and individual.

All who listened participated. Those who read this are encouraged to take four sheets of paper and complete them as described above.

He concluded by quoting from a book of readings that he received when he participated in an Outward Bound program in a wilderness area:

"If I had to live my life over again, I'd dare to make more mistakes next time . . . I would take more trips, climb more mountains, swim more rivers . . . Oh, I've had my moments. And if I had it to do over again, I'd try to have more of them. I would go to more dances . . . I would pick more daisies."

- Nadine Stair

Charles R. "Red" Scott

The Nation, In Decline, Needs A Thinker Like Jefferson

(Published July 4, 1987)

During the early 1960's, in a room full of Nobel Prize winners, President Kennedy noted that this was probably the greatest assemblage of brainpower in the White House since the author of the Declaration of Independence, Thomas Jefferson, dined alone. Jefferson's accomplishments reached into many fields; his bold yet quiet effectiveness earned him his place as one of America's most outstanding individuals.

After Jefferson wrote one of the most important documents in human history, which we celebrate today, it took the Revolutionary War and some social and political experimentation before our Constitution was signed. A constructive tension was established, symbolized by the Declaration calling for freedom and the Constitution providing laws and obligations necessary to maintain that freedom. Creative, positive change and sacrifice thus became vital parts of our heritage.

Succeeding generations of Americans have done what was necessary to develop opportunities, overcome adversities, and advance the common faith that this is a nation trying to provide all of its citizens with the right of "Life, Liberty, and the Pursuit of Happiness." Throughout our history, freedom or its requirements, or an evolving blend, dominated our culture.

Whenever that culture applied all of its moral, political, economic, and military capabilities, this country became pre-eminent in the world - at war and at peace. Working together with our individual and collective will, we triumphed as a people and as proponents of freedom. Whenever we have not used all of our resources - at war or at peace - we have not achieved our objectives.

We seem to have slipped recently. There has been a decline in our relative economic power. Within a few years, we have gone from the world's largest creditor to its largest debtor. Thirty years ago, the United States had 15 of the world's largest banks; today, we have two of the top 25. Japan has 14, including all of the four largest. Materialism and consumerism, unconnected to a higher purpose, weave through our society. One would think that Americans fought and died to make the world safe for credit cards and designer labels. Our foreign policy is challenged at home and abroad. Self-sufficiency and our ability to control our destiny are an illusion. In short, we have been losing our edge.

We have gone a little too far along the pendulum of exercising and enjoying our freedom, and now need to do what is required to be assured of maintaining it. An educated, imaginative citizenry, which we must work to develop, combined with the right leadership, can go forward with vigor and vision, and correct our course.

Regarding leadership, we would be well served to try to identify someone with capability and perspective, someone like Thomas Jefferson. As to perspective, he viewed his contribution to education and his writing of the Declaration of Independence as being far more significant than serving as governor, secretary of state, and even as president of the United States.

The anonymous American who wrote the following understood how to require and inspire, as did Thomas Jefferson, and as does freedom:

"Do not follow where the path may lead. Go instead, where there is no path, and leave a trail."

Thomas Jefferson
AP/WIDE WORLD PHOTOS.

Historian Paul Kennedy Sees A New World Order Emerging

(Published May 21, 1988)

Best-selling author and history professor Paul Kennedy gave the annual Silver lecture a few weeks ago at Columbia University's School of International and Public Affairs. Dwight Eisenhower, George Marshall, Anthony Eden, Abba Eban, Rajiv Gandhi and Helmut Schmidt spoke in prior years. Kennedy also met with the school's advisory board to discuss his ideas.

Since January, when his book, "The Rise and Fall of the Great Powers," was published, Kennedy has been in demand as government and business leaders, educators, and others have sought his insights. *The New York Times Book Review* recognized his thoughts as "of almost Toynbeean sweep." His views are straightforward, interrelated, and important enough to merit consideration, and hopefully, encourage positive action. Some of the highlights of his discussions at Columbia go beyond the points made in his book.

First, he reviews the last 500 years of history and noted how one great power after another declined after its military obligations and foreign commitments overextended its economic base; each did not realign its obligations with capacities. Portugal, Spain and England all fell victim to a similar fate as their reach exceeded their grasp.

Secondly, he credits a few far-sighted people in the latter 15 years of the 19th century with correctly predicting the 20th century importance of this country, due to evidence of our growing economic and technological achievements. Accordingly, he acknowledged the "echo of history" and predicts that at least several countries in the Far East will emerge in the 21st century because of strengths currently exhibited.

As those "Asian tigers come of age," he anticipates a world of multipolar, rather than bipolar, power. He specifically foresees five significant spheres of influence by the year 2000 - the United States, China, Japan, the Soviet Union, and an integrated Western Europe. He believes that the international order will look quite different and that a major reconsideration of relationships will occur. NATO and other alliances that have been very relevant in this century may be expected to change or even disappear in what he sees as "a New World order."

Perhaps most importantly, Kennedy calls attention to the choice that we have now. Unless a number of trends and policies are altered, our country faces steady, relative decline compared to certain other nations. He is clear that we are not predetermined to decline; however, he states that other great powers historically have not taken the corrective policy options available to them. As they lacked the will to take concrete measures to change, and as they postponed tough choices, they lost their position of greatness over time.

The characteristics of indications of national success that he identifies are a high savings rate and strong commitments to education, science, design, and technological innovation. Unless the erosion of our economic and related cultural foundations is reversed, Kennedy's theory is that our relative world position will decline in the next century. He recommends a number of actions, including having our allies bear more of the cost of their defense and increasing the length of the school year to a number closer to the 240-day school year in Japan.

History does not stand still; for a great nation and people to remain such, according to Kennedy, their economic and scientific capabilities must continue to lead the world over time. In the words of former British Prime Minister and Silver lecturer Anthony Eden, "Every succeeding scientific discovery makes greater nonsense of old-time conceptions of sovereignty."

Barbara Bush's Advice: Cherish Your Human Connections

(Published June 23, 1990)

Constant change has become as certain as death and taxes in our time. Unexpected developments are taking place in many aspects of our lives, including in international relations, as the world is transformed. Recurring questions are asked such as, "What does America need to do to retain its strength on this changing planet?" "What enduring values transcend all of this change?"

Within the last few weeks alone, Soviet President Gorbachev articulated that "the Cold War is now behind us," as the superpower summit concluded. President Carlos Salinas de Gortari of Mexico visited Washington to begin negotiations to fashion a free-trade agreement that could lead to a North American Common Market comparable to the forthcoming economic unification of Europe. Leaders of Greece and East Germany, among others met with our president during recent weeks to discuss evolving conditions in their respective countries. Further, Nelson Mandela continues his courageous quest to end apartheid in South Africa as he tours our country.

While these major headlines and excerpts from various leaders' remarks capture our attention, perhaps the most insightful and memorable words of this season were articulated by someone whose personal leadership qualities were questioned until earlier this month. Notwithstanding some prominent competition, my candidate for "Best Statesperson and Leader" so far this decade is Barbara Bush.

On June 3, Mrs. Bush spoke at the Wellesley College commencement. A vocal minority of students protested her invitation to speak on the grounds that her only accomplishment in life was marrying someone who became president of the United States. She was criticized as not being a leader in her own right. These protestors wanted an additional speaker "who would more aptly reflect the self-affirming qualities" of the school's graduates. Being an effective spouse and capable parent were insufficient for these protestors.

Because of the controversy, Mrs. Bush's speech received significant attention. It was a triumph for Mrs. Bush as, in addition to winning over her audience, she demonstrated an aspect of real leadership in personifying and articulating that worldly success is no more important than being truly committed to family and friends. She communicated thoughtful counsel that may focus us on vital priorities in these changing and challenging times - developing and nurturing capable individuals whose generation will follow us and being loyal to our friends.

With open-mindedness, graciousness, and good humor, Mrs. Bush affirmed that being a solid person, friend, and parent is as important as any other accomplishment. By recognizing that a person's character is his destiny and that those parents who are devoted to encouraging their children's growth are unsung heroes, Barbara Bush projected the most important of "self-affirming qualities." Amidst phenomenal change, Barbara Bush exemplified the fact that one thing will never change for fathers and mothers; if you have children, they come first; if you have true friends, you must be one. Only with such parental dedication and involvement, and with such commitment to our friends and fellow citizens, will we sustain the values that keep us strong as individuals and as a country.

Accordingly, while a number of statements will be made by world leaders on a number of important subjects to help us understand and to influence events in our changing times, the following words from Mrs. Bush's address are certain to have lasting importance:

"Cherish your human connections, as your relationship with family and friends .. as important as your obligations as a doctor, a lawyer, a business leader will be . . . those human connections with spouses, with children, with friends are the most important investment you will ever make.

At the end of your life, you will never regret not having passed one more test, winning one more verdict, or not closing one more deal. You will regret time not spent with a husband, a child, a friend, or a parent."

Barbara Bush (Wellesley College Commencement Speaker)
AP/WIDE WORLD PHOTOS.

Margaret Thatcher's Advice: Don't Be Wobbly

(Published April 27, 1991)

"Don't be wobbly," were her now-famous words as she buttressed President Bush's instinct last August to "not let Saddam Hussein's aggression stand." Former British Prime Minister Margaret Thatcher spoke and acted in the manner that has punctuated her distinguished career. She rejected the inevitability of the unacceptable, and acted upon the strength of her philosophy and convictions. She didn't wait for opinion polls to determine her position.

When she resigned last November, *The Wall Street Journal* in an editorial entitled, "A Woman of Some Importance," said, "it took a special inspiration to stand athwart history in the first place, to reject the inevitability of decline that so many accepted. Mrs. Thatcher's was a distinctively British form of greatness . . ." Her remarkable career produced an era of significant change and rejuvenation in Britain as she implemented her philosophy of a strong free market economy, privatization of state enterprises, and broad-based tax reductions. She has been a dependable friend of the United States, and acclaims it as a model of what personal freedom can achieve.

She had the distinction of serving as Prime Minister for almost 12 consecutive years, and was the first person to so serve since the early part of the 19th century. Almost no one would argue that she and Winston Churchill are the two outstanding British Prime Ministers of this century. The two are among the few people who shaped world events during this period of history.

Accordingly, for someone who has been an Anglo-phile since being a student there, and who believes that equality of women's rights is natural and not an issue, a recent private meeting with Margaret Thatcher was a very special experience. While a wide range of subjects was discussed, several observations may be of interest and appropriate herein.

Most importantly, she is a truly amazing lady with great personal strengths and abilities. It is very reassuring to know that someone of exceptional competence, not a media myth creation, can be a leader in our modern Western world. She possesses classic personal attributes for being outstanding. She is well educated, intelligent, hard working, and has a keen sense of responsibility rooted in clear and solid values. Her speaking and debating skills are a testament to the importance of those capabilities in a public leader. She is knowledgeable on many subjects, with an impressive command of detail; she is evidently well read.

She is forthright and does what she says she will do. She lives by her commitments and does not waiver. She does not believe that a person or a government should spend more than is received. She left office with a budget surplus. She changed her country and influenced the world by courageously and consistently advancing policies based on a clear sense of right and wrong. She stood for something.

When she speaks of "ethical capitalism," she expresses a genuine belief that only an economic system based upon free enterprise and ethical principles can meet the needs of people over time. Her economic position is based upon thought and conviction, and not upon a desire to defend life-long privilege. To the contrary, her upbringing was one of modest circumstances.

Margaret Thatcher is as engaging in conversation as she is formidable in debate. Her strength of character and conviction are irrepressible and instantly apparent. She is gracious, articulate, vigorous, and inspiring as only a person of true accomplishment and confidence can be. She is truly a tour de force.

She is going through a period of change and transition in her life. One has the clear feeling, however, that she will continue to be effective and powerful on a number of levels. She may be called on again by the British in a similar way as Churchill was asked to return after his defeat at the end of World War II. She may contribute in any of a number of other ways on the world scene. For sure, whatever she does, Margaret Thatcher will never, ever "be wobbly."

Lady Margaret Thatcher
AP/WIDE WORLD PHOTOS.

Bill Clinton Lives Up To His Promise As A Rhodes Scholar

(Published January 2, 1993)

Almost one year ago today, a column by this writer suggested that the election of 1992 would be "a turning point in American history." It anticipated George Bush's electoral loss at a time when polls and pundits viewed him as unbeatable. The election of 1992 was a turning point in many ways and will result in change, which will officially begin early in this new year.

When viewed by future generations, one of the most remarkable aspects of the recent election will be the ascendancy to the presidency of the United State of the first person to emerge from America's competitive educational merit system - "our edumeritocracy." Bill Clinton will be America's first president who was a Rhodes Scholar. Other honors and forms of recognition exist; a Rhodes Scholarship, however, is acknowledged as the pre-eminent award.

Election as a Rhodes Scholar has confirmed recognition of promise of greatness for those college graduates who are chosen. Thirty-two outstanding students are elected annually, who then study at Oxford University in England. Selection criteria include literacy and scholastic attainments, compassion for the less fortunate, interest and ability in sports, and moral force of character and instincts to lead. Rhodes Scholars have been successful in many fields, including government. Some have been U.S. senators and congressmen, Supreme Court justices, and Cabinet members, including secretary of state and attorney general. My personal experience confirms their capability for outstanding accomplishment. A graduate school roommate, Bob McKelvey, was a Rhodes Scholar a few years before Clinton; he excelled at whatever he did.

Some of the characteristics of a Rhodes Scholar are those needed by a president at this point in America's history. They include energy, accomplishment-orientation, tenacity, intelligence, problem-solving ability, and the courage to take on a challenge. For the first time, an individual who was pre-selected in his youth on the basis of talent and ability to fulfill great promise will hold the nation's highest office. That individual earned recognition while a young person as a Rhodes Scholar with promise; he now has the opportunity to fulfill that promise by his performance as president when the country needs exceptional leadership to address its problems and remain the world's leader.

While election as a Rhodes Scholar proferred the probability of success, many have not fulfilled their potential. Frequently, it was lack of tenacity and boldness in career pursuits that was the reason. Bill Clinton has no such weaknesses; while he has others, his pursuit of the presidency against seemingly impossible odds reflects this determination, confidence - and luck. All of these qualities can serve him and our country well.

Accordingly, the promise of Bill Clinton's youth, combined with his experiences, augur well for his performance as president. This fundamental change regarding the nature of the person who will be president is a turning point in our nation's history. No family wealth, connections, or assistance were relevant in his election as Rhodes Scholar and as president.

Expectations for the first "edumeritocrat" to be president are high. Short-term disappointments are inevitable. The problems that he is expected to solve have developed over a long time, and are likely not to be resolvable in Clinton's first 100 days, or perhaps, in his first several years.

Nonetheless, this is a self-described "different kind of Democrat" who looks to Thomas Jefferson for both inauguration symbolism and policy inspiration. We shall be well-served if President Clinton demonstrates some of Jefferson's abilities and adheres to his ideals as he projects his own unique blend of Oxford sophistication and Hope, Ark., country manner, common sense and straight talk.

Bill Clinton's conduct, especially at his economic conference a few weeks ago, has been reassuring. A number of his appointments have been inspired. If he can use these outstanding abilities which were honed in our educational system and first recognized when he was elected a Rhodes Scholar, all Americans, including the majority who did not vote for him, will benefit. Hopefully, the promise of his youth will be fulfilled by his performance as president and will be so recognized in his and our time - well before the judgment of future generations.

President William Jefferson Clinton
AP/WIDE WORLD PHOTOS.

Courter Rendered Great Service On Base Closing Panel

(Published July 10, 1993)

Four summers ago, a Feedback column by this writer recalled "a conversation at a reunion with a college classmate . . . a congressman from New Jersey. He is deeply interested in the issues facing the nation. . and has plans to address them." He ran for governor of New Jersey and lost, in part because of federal abortion policies which had limited place in a gubernatorial election and which were "out of proportion to the totality of public concerns." The column concluded with, "what finally happens this November in New Jersey is of consequence for us."

That classmate did not attend this year's reunion in early June. He was here in Corpus Christi and in other places during that time. His name is Jim Courter; he was serving as chairman of the Defense Base Closure and Realignment Commission (the Commission).

It is an ironic comment on our time that Jim Courter is closer to addressing one of the key "issues facing the nation" after his elective political career ended than many politicians are after their victory. The commission's recommendations, approved by the president, must now be accepted or rejected as an entire package by Congress.

Jim Courter's public service on the commission is proving far more effective than is the experience of many of those who are serving in elected political office. The commission focused on one problem, resolved it, and thereby provided an example of how to obtain results on an important public concern in this era of unresponsive national government.

The commission was formed because our political system couldn't accomplish necessary military downsizing. The commission is an independent body, which was empowered to investigate and recommend a course of action. It conscientiously and capably analyzed the alternatives and reached conclusions which, closely but not completely, conformed to the original recommendations of military professionals - irrespective of considerable political pressure during the process.

The system has shown itself to be institutionally incapable of addressing essential, fundamental long-term issues. A mechanism was crafted to break the political stalemate, but still allow review by elected officials. The president and members of Congress retain the power to accept or reject the conclusions, but they cannot "play politics," horse-trade, or make changes. The purpose is to obtain results in our national interest, not just the interest of a community, region, or narrow concern - either ours or someone else's.

This is a period of phenomenal, fundamental change in so many aspects of life around the world; yet, we are unable to change the direction of most of our domestic problems despite electoral promises and our expectations. Business as usual isn't working in these areas. Elected officials struggle to truly lead and expend much of their effort mediating among competing interest groups. The American people are losing confidence in their government's ability to solve those problems for which it has clear responsibility and for which it has appropriated the financial resources by taxing us.

The commission has served as a successful instrument of change that actually addressed an important public issue. What other domestic initiative of real consequence has become a reality recently? Our fast-moving society is becoming increasingly disconnected from our slow and non-moving political institutions. Until these institutions and their leaders function more effectively, we may want to consider, create, and empower other commissions. Competent, independent, non-politically motivated citizens could address other vital and sensitive areas, which are now deadlocked in political stalemate and ideological rhetoric, such as entitlements, deficit reduction, and stronger anti-violent crime measures. With more homeless people than at any time since the Depression and many public schools in disarray, empowered citizen commissions would be preferable to institutional paralysis or abandonment. The commission was an experiment that worked in the best interest of our country. It may now serve as an example of how to resolve other previously intractable problems.

You Never Stop Learning From A Gifted And Talented Teacher

(Published October 23, 1993)

Is there anyone among us who would not like to return to an earlier time in his or her life for awhile? "You can't go home again," Thomas Wolfe told us. Nonetheless, when an opportunity is so afforded, it can be especially rewarding.

Such was my experience a few weeks ago when a former graduate school professor of mine gave a lecture that I attended. As he did a generation ago, Dr. John Stoessinger placed international affairs and life into an insightful perspective. Other than our parents, teachers at all levels of education can best prepare and inspire us to utilize our talents and lead our lives more fully and productively.

Some educators, like Dr. Stoessinger, go far beyond individual teaching in their impact. Dr. Stoessinger is currently Distinguished Professor of International Affairs at Trinity University in San Antonio. He previously taught at Harvard, M.I.T., Columbia, and Princeton. He also is a prize-winning author of important books on world politics. His "The Might of Nations: World Politics in Our Time" won the Bancroft Prize for history when first published; it is still the leading textbook used in college-level courses in international affairs. He holds a doctorate from Harvard where his classmates included Henry Kissinger and Zbigniew Brzezinski.

Kissinger and Brzezinski reached pinnacles in their careers in positions of action, i.e., as practitioners of international affairs. Kissinger was secretary of state under President Nixon and Brzezinski was national security adviser under President Carter. Traditionally, people of action are more highly venerated and receive more public recognition in our society. Stoessinger has been more of a person of the book, of thoughts, and of reflection. It is arguable as to which contributions will have the most lasting and deepest impact - those which involved the more visible world of action or those which involved the more under-heralded world of thought and reflection.

Much of what I and others learned as students of Dr. Stoessinger in the 1960s has been of value ever since. For example, he introduced recognition of the distinction between image and reality in understanding international and interpersonal relations.

Further, in his book "The United Nations and the Superpowers," he illuminated the idea that the United Nations was not only an idealistic forum of nations, but also a practical participant in power politics. It offered a mechanism to be used by nations to advance their interests. Accordingly, the United States has withheld paying its dues when we viewed the United Nations as not advancing our foreign policy interests rather than paying for an "ideal" defined by others. A teacher-analyst of this ability can have a considerable influence on events as they happen in addition to analyzing them after the fact.

In his recent lecture, Dr. Stoessinger focused on Russia and China as most important for American international interests generally, and the most promising for American business interests specifically. He called the birth of freedom in Russia the most important international event in the latter half of the 20th century. He cautioned that our current preoccupation with domestic issues like health care reform would be quickly overshadowed if freedom fails in Russia and Cold War II is commenced.

He believes that future historians will see communism in China as a transitional phase to recover the country from prior foreign domination. Until the current elderly generation of Chinese leaders passes, he sees China as authoritarian, but with a growing free market economy. He calls China "The Klondike of the 1990s." He also believes that we can learn much from its ancient civilization and "age" culture.

Dr. Stoessinger is an outstanding and gifted teacher. One aspect of his lectures remains the same. As a child, he fled Nazi-occupied Europe through Siberia to China, where he lived his teen-age years. He never fails to express his gratitude to the United States for the freedom and opportunity it provided him, and to make us aware of how fortunate we are to live here. He also reminds us of our responsibility to future generations to contribute to solving the problems of the world's greatest democracy.

No matter where we are in our lives, or how much time has passed since we were students, we can go to class again!

Dr. John Stoessinger

Carter's Greatest Role Came After Defeat

(Published October 15, 1994)

It's not over until it's over. These words from competitive sports may also refer to ultimate judgments about a president of the United States who left office after losing re-election by a wide margin - Jimmy Carter.

In the summer of 1980, Carter's last year as president, a public opinion poll showed only 21 percent of Americans approved of his performance; it was the lowest rating of any president on record.

Carter's principal priority, a domestic agenda, was thwarted, in large measure, by international developments, including the oil cartel. Gasoline shortages, high inflation, and high interest rates at home were exacerbated by events abroad with the Iran hostage crisis and the Soviet invasion of Afghanistan.

As we approach the 21st century, some perspective seems appropriate. History will surely be more kind to Jimmy Carter than the times in which he served as president. In fact, he may be the most outstanding ex-president of the century.

Jimmy Carter is emerging as one of today's most respected public figures. We witness today the success of his recent mission to Haiti. It continues a post-presidential career as peacemaker, election monitor in foreign countries, advocate and carpenter for the homeless, and innovator in seeking solutions to social problems that plague poor families. The Carter Center in Atlanta sponsors projects to revitalize inner cities.

He has worked toward peaceful resolution of conflicts with Castro of Cuba and Kim of North Korea.

On occasion, he may be criticized for going too far to avoid military action, such as when he opposed the Gulf War, but he has been consistent in trying to do all within his personal ability to avoid war and conflict.

His efforts have sometimes been at substantial personal risk. Amidst all this, he has written a book of poetry, "Always a Reckoning," to be published early next year.

How does one reconcile these contradictory images of a failed presidency and a successful ex-presidency of public service? One of the ironies is that the same characteristics that have led to Carter's success as an ex-president contributed to his problems as president. His earnest, personal hands-on commitment has been at the heart of many of his recent accomplishments. It is reminiscent of his single greatest achievement as president, the Camp David agreement. Detailed focus, or micromanagement, can be effective when one can focus on a single issue at a time, as can an ex-president. As president, these same characteristics interfere with setting priorities and focusing on the big picture, as required in the nation's highest office.

Jimmy Carter's policies as president were based upon a belief that there is a role for government to play to make the lives of ordinary citizens better.

It is ironic that some of his greatest contributions to that objective came as a private citizen, both in deed and by example.

For some exceptionally motivated people, like former President Jimmy Carter, it isn't over until after it's over.

President Jimmy Carter
AP/WIDE WORLD PHOTOS.

Japanese Risked Their Lives To Save Others

(Published August 19, 1995)

Sometimes, we learn from truly gifted and talented teachers at unexpected times. Such lessons may be provided even before classes begin in the new school year in South Texas. In addition to having students acquire factual knowledge, important objectives of teachers and education generally are to reinforce character development and to encourage critical thinking and independent judgment.

A former teacher of mine recently participated in a footnote in history and in so doing continued to provide valuable lessons in these areas which are the purposes of education. The greater historical context is timely this week as we mark the 50th anniversary of Japan's surrender in World War II. We are familiar with that time in history, including Japanese war atrocities and the extraordinary bravery, dedication and sacrifice of that generation of Americans.

This teacher, Dr. John Stoessinger (of whom I wrote in a Feedback column last year) was born in Vienna. He spent his childhood as a refugee from the Nazi Holocaust. Fleeing Vienna to Prague, his family obtained a visa to Shanghai through the Soviet Union/Siberia and Japan. He survived the war in Shanghai and then came to the United States after V-J Day with the assistance of an American soldier. He received his doctorate from Harvard at the same time as Henry Kissinger and Zbigniew Brzezinski and became part of an influential foreign-born, foreign policy elite in the United States. His "The Might of Nations: World Politics in Our Time" won the Bancroft Prize for History when first published; it is still the leading textbook used in college-level courses in international affairs.

After the war, the Stoessinger family learned that their lives had been saved on two separate circumstances by two Japanese diplomats, each of whom acted at great personal risk and against prevailing orders. Dr. Stoessinger tried to track down the two people who were responsible for their escape, but was unable to find them.

Recently, Dr. Stoessinger gave a speech in Kobe, Japan, and asked the press corps if they could provide assistance. A reporter for a leading Japanese newspaper, the *Kobe Shimbun,* identified the two diplomats, Consul Chiune Sugihara and Dr. Ryoichi Manabe, who had helped the Stoessingers and many others by their courageous personal actions. Each of these unheralded and previously unrecognized heroes was like a Japanese Oskar Schindler or Raoul Wallenberg. At a defining time in their lives, they took independent action at considerable risk.

Sugihara died in disgrace in1986. When faced with the choice between his conscience and wrongful orders from his government, he followed his conscience. He was rehabilitated after his death.

Dr. Manabe was found living alone in Tokyo at age 87 with an unlisted phone number. Dr. Stoessinger flew there to see him and arranged a reception to honor him and two others that had helped those who could not help themselves at the risk of their own lives. Dr. Stoessinger's experience, and his finding and expressing good in the ranks of a former enemy, became a footnote to history.

Dr. Stoessinger, like all great teachers, continues to teach in the classroom and in life. As he wrote this summer, "There is no such thing as collective guilt, and, in dark times, there are always men and women who will confront evil, even in its most absolute form, and reaffirm our humanity. In the depths of the abyss, moral courage still survives and at times even prevails."

John Updike Entertains 'Rabbit' Fans

(Published November 25, 1995)

Two exceptional events took place last week in different parts of our country. One was the announcement that two 17-year-old twins in Chamblee, Ga., were the first twins ever to score 1600 - the highest possible - on their Scholastic Aptitude Tests. Their mother credited their being avid and diverse readers from early childhood as essential to their success.

Another was the visit to Corpus Christi by a true American literary hero, Pulitzer Prize-winning author John Updike. Those who met or heard him received a treat as they learned that at least one world-class writer is a warm, engaging person whose manner will make further reading of his work even more enjoyable.

What do these diverse events have in common? In this age of television, computers, computer games, VCRs, and emerging cyberspace, the above demonstrate that the value and joy of reading is alive. Those who develop a real love for reading, especially at a young age, stand to reap a lifetime of benefit in both tangible competitive performance and, more importantly, personal growth, pleasure and insight. Reading instructs and delights.

One distinguished educator at a leading university greeted this fall's freshman class with the observation that the best advice that he ever received and, accordingly, could offer to them was to try to read a book a week. Reading as much, as often, and as broadly possible is as important, if not more so, in the new information age, which is replacing the industrial and agricultural ages in world history. While information may be easily accessible, the key will be exercising informed judgment in many different and changing situations. The ability to discern what is vital and to use organized, readily available facts and knowledge most productively can best be developed by reading extensively.

As a citizen of this country, every American has the opportunity and right to become as capable, successful and contributing a person as he or she is able. Continuing education, buttressed by reading, may be the most effective affirmative action program.

In this world of limitless potential and diversity, reading supplements and enhances our direct experiences. From studying the origin of the universe and exploring outer space to pursuing mutually exclusive lifestyles and careers, we simply cannot do everything first hand; reading provides surrogate participation in greater and more meaningful depth than sound bites and summaries. Further, in a time of globalization, reading about different cultures and human adventures and activities makes us more receptive, tolerant and understanding of others.

We can read and learn about other people, whether it be their intense, personal struggles or their wealth of common sense or understated wit and humor. Reading provides insights and perspective into our lives and circumstances; we can expand our levels of understanding and sense of personal destiny and purpose.

As a nation, we can read about the outstanding civilizations that were the world leaders in their time as America is today, and learn why they declined. Rome, Byzantium, and others lost their spiritual compass and sense of dedication as well as their military superiority. When they stopped passing on the qualities of excellence to succeeding generations, in part by ceasing to emphasize reading, they diminished their character and will to adhere to the values of their past greatness.

Accordingly, the place for reading in America as we move toward a new century with new technologies and possibilities is as significant as ever.

John Updike (author)
AP/WIDE WORLD PHOTOS.

Reston Was The Best Journalist Of His Time

(Published January 13, 1996)

In this century . . . "the U.S. doesn't seem to be able to make necessary decisions without a crisis deadline." This certainly describes Washington today.

However, this was written several years ago by someone who was widely regarded as the most influential journalist of his generation - James "Scotty" Reston.

The ability to communicate such lasting relevant insight contributed to his winning two Pulitzer Prizes for reporting along with many other honors during the half century that he was with the *New York Times* from 1939 to 1989.

This Washington-based journalistic legend interviewed and wrote about most of the world's leaders during his time. His columns were required reading for many people, especially those in positions of power. He often wrote about the challenge of change, which he called "the central issue of our age."

Born in Scotland, Reston was a most articulate patriot for his adopted country until his death five weeks ago. He concluded his last column as a full-time columnist with: "I'm going to try to bring back the smoke-filled room so that the next presidential candidates will be chosen by people who know something about them. . finally, I'm going to write a long love letter to America."

He was moderate and non-partisan. "I never thought that either party had the key to the Promised Land." He viewed public officials as "no worse today that they used to be, but the reporting is better."

Reston's style was one of clarity, directness, and humor; he wrote with great eloquence, but with simple sentences. His perspective was original and engaging. He noted that "Kissinger not only knows a lot about foreign affairs, he is a foreign affair." About the presidency, he said that "it lifts one fallible mortal from many millions and says: Go guide half the human race. No wonder people pray . . ." He said that his approach to his columns was "to write a letter to a friend who doesn't have the time to find out all the goofy things that go on in Washington."

Reston believed that great leaders would make history and change the nation by their decisive actions. "If George Washington had waited for the doubters, he'd still be crossing the Delaware." Also, "Lyndon Johnson is to the politics of America what the state of Texas is to other states . . . a gargantuan figure."

Part of my interest in writing was motivated by the respect and regard that I had for "Scotty" Reston, whose columns I began to read as a college freshman.

Reston brilliantly expressed an enlightened optimism about America, life, and even death. He concluded his book of personal memoirs, "Deadline," with this thought: "I do not fear death itself for I find consolation in feeling a part of the life that has gone before and in the lives of our children and our grandchildren that will continue when we are gone."

Journalist James "Scotty" Reston
AP/WIDE WORLD PHOTOS.

Outstanding Americans Inspire Us All

(Published May 17, 1997)

The 50th Annual Horatio Alger Award Activities were held in Washington, D.C. a few weeks ago. Ten outstanding Americans who overcame considerable obstacles to achieve success were recognized. They included businessman John Huntsman and Carlos Cantu, author Mary Higgins Clark, actor James Earl Jones, and media leader Ted Turner.

Their life stories and accomplishments were very moving and inspirational; the ceremonies will be nationally broadcast on PBS next month.

Among a number of outstanding speakers during the activities, Maya Angelou, a former Horatio Alger Award recipient, 1992 Inaugural Poet, and a distinguished author and professor, was exceptionally memorable.

She expressed a wish that there would not need to be a 100th anniversary of an organization the purposes of which are to recognize those adults who have triumphed over adversity and to assist a number of very challenged students to obtain a college education. She hoped that there would be no need in 50 years because the underlying conditions that created such adversity for young people would no longer exist.

Maya Angelou certainly focused attention on what needs to be done to address some of society's most significant problems. Strengthening family values, emphasizing the ethic of responsibility, encouraging civility and concern for others, diminishing selfishness, and building communities where people care for each other rather than practice marksmanship are goals toward which she pointed us.

She spoke of "rainbows in the clouds," referring to those people who help the less fortunate when all seems dark. She commended those who volunteer to assist those in need and give back to their communities. "Not the crowd's roar nor the tiniest gasps of the timid can stay their mission. They encourage us to be more than we ever dreamed we could be . . ."

She concluded by saying "that courage is the most important part of all virtues." Without minimizing other great aspects of character, she noted that, without courage, the other virtues couldn't be attained. It has taken, and will require, acts of personal courage, to create the environment within which the other virtues can be developed and sustained. Moral courage is that which can most effect constructive change; doing the right thing is what has differentiated America as a country and what has distinguished truly admirable people throughout history.

South Texas has been home to a number of such courageous people - Presidential Medal of Freedom recipient Dr. Hector Garcia, World War II decorated hero Joe Dawson, and many others who have demonstrated this virtue either in difficult and exceptional circumstances, or in leading their daily lives, or both. King High School Principal Sherry Blackett exhibited this kind of courage recently when she risked a contempt of court conviction for maintaining confidentiality for students who trusted her by coming forth with information at great personal risk.

"Without courage, you cannot practice any other virtue consistently, not consistently. You can be sometimes kind, sometimes fair, sometimes generous, and even sometimes loving, but consistently without courage, one can't be anything very much." - Maya Angelou.

Another Death Merits At Least A Footnote

(Published September 13, 1997)

The deaths of Diana, Princess of Wales, and Mother Teresa have been well chronicled throughout the world with tributes to their exceptional, respective lives. Ironically, limited attention was given to another person who died last week whose life work partially explains the extraordinary public outpouring of sympathy, caring, and grief for these two women. Accordingly, it seems appropriate to recognize Dr. Victor Frankl of Vienna.

Dr. Frankl was one of the pioneers of modern psychology and psychiatry; he was a brilliant analyst of human behavior. He first used the term "existentialism" and emphasized leading our lives rather than asking questions about the meaning of life. "We need to stop asking ourselves about the meaning of life and to think of ourselves as those who are being questioned by life - daily and hourly."

He recommended facing and dealing with life courageously and directly. His "Man's Search for Meaning" was named one of the most influential books in America by the Library of Congress and was one of the best-selling books of the last 50 years.

Dr. Frankl foresaw and contributed to explaining why people become so engaged and involved in the lives of others in our modern times - including those distant from us. His theories foreshadowed, even predicted, the intense personal interest in certain public figures and celebrities which was demonstrated so extraordinarily in the last two weeks as hundreds of millions of people, on a world-wide basis, were immersed in genuine grief for two people that they did not personally know. Contemporary communications can account for part of this phenomenon, but Frankl obviously recognized something in the human soul that would respond in this way.

His original thinking combined with his experience as a World War II concentration camp survivor provided the intellectual and real life foundation for hundreds of popular self-help books. He believed that people have the will power and freedom of choice to handle their problems. He was positive and hopeful despite terrible personal adversity. He believed that people should find significance and meaning in the individual circumstances of their own lives - whatever they may be, that is the key to psychological strength.

It is more than an irony that a person who was one of the greatest original thinkers and analysts of people's conduct and values in the 20th century, who helped us understand the quest for meaning in life and left an enduring legacy of distinction and accomplishment, received only modest attention at his death last week. It is a statement about us and our society, one that Victor Frankl would be the first to recognize and understand.

It is clear that Mother Teresa and Princess Diana will long be remembered in the recorded history of our time. Victor Frankl should at least merit a footnote.

Mother Teresa, Princess Diana
AP/WIDE WORLD PHOTOS.

Tommy Thompson Shows How Politics Can Work

(Published May 16, 1998)

"I try to help people help themselves. That is why I got involved in welfare reform. It was paying people not to work, not to get married, and to have more children. There was no accountability . . . Maintaining the status quo is the same thing as moving backwards."

These are some of the thoughts communicated in Washington a few weeks ago by Gov. Tommy Thompson of Wisconsin. He was one of 10 new members inducted into the Horatio Alger Association of Distinguished Americans at its annual awards ceremonies. It was refreshing to be in the nation's capital and hear a prominent public figure discuss issues and ideas without partisanship or politics.

Thompson is the first governor in Wisconsin's history to be elected to three four-year terms. He strives to obtain results in a non-partisan, co-operative manner. He is recognized as the person who initiated welfare reform in America. Federal welfare reform is based on Wisconsin's pioneering initiatives, led by Gov. Thompson.

Wisconsin has reduced its welfare caseload more than any other state in the country. He is highly regarded for his political courage and leadership in taking risks to fix what doesn't work. He believes that people should have the opportunity to live the American Dream rather than face a future of limited hope and despair.

His approach is hands-on. Thompson said that he gets his best ideas from those most directly affected. He also solicits feedback from people participating in the process.

He recalled hosting a lunch for 10 women who had been on welfare. One woman in particular had a real sense of dignity and self respect that came from working for the first time and being promoted. She was especially proud that her employer gave her a pager because she had become so important to the business that he needed to be able to reach her at all times.

Some politicians pursue re-election rather than solutions. Whether welfare reform, educational improvement, or other important issues, Thompson recognizes that initiating and effecting change is difficult and politically risky. He takes risks for what he believes and says that; "some people swallow something sour in the morning, chew lemons all day, and behave accordingly." Their negative, do-nothing, approach needs to be successfully challenged by positive, forward-looking people.

One might ask what motivated Thompson to attack welfare reform, a primarily urban problem, when he grew up in a small Midwestern farming community. He says that his hometown, "is so small that you can call somebody, get a wrong number, and still talk for half an hour." But this spirit of a close-knit community encourages an attitude of wanting to help people. That is why he chose public life - to make a real difference in people's lives.

His advice for those similarly motivated: "Believe in yourself and don't be afraid to take risks. Even if you fail, at least you tried."

Gov. Tommy Thompson of Wisconsin
AP/WIDE WORLD PHOTOS.

Extraordinary Leaders Show Perserverance And A Clear Vision

(Published July 25, 1998)

Students of human behavior believe that many, if not most, people are uncertain about their personal goals or objectives. Since they are not sure of where they want to be, it is obviously difficult to get there. Those with clear vision have the advantage of focus and dedicated direction, which increase the probability of success.

During the first 10 days of this month, our family saw several successful, extraordinary individuals: Robert Redford in Sundance, Utah; Dr. John Mendelsohn and other key members of the cancer research team from M.D. Anderson Hospital of Houston; and former President George Bush in Kennebunkport, Maine. We admired their accomplishments in such diverse areas as the arts, science, and government, but were even more struck by what they appeared to share in common.

Each of these extraordinary leaders demonstrated qualities of focus and concentration of effort and energy over the long period of their careers; they knew what they wanted. While several changed career direction early as they obtained greater personal clarity, commitment and dedication remain their common hallmark. Each was also motivated by making a difference and by a sense of higher purpose. All were prepared during younger stages of their lives through education or relevant experience, or both, for the positions in which they have excelled.

To many, Robert Redford is a true motion picture icon as an actor and director, but he has also dedicated much of his life and resources to advancing the arts and the environment. For almost three decades, he has built Sundance, Utah, into one of the world's finest homes for theater, arts, arts education, and development of emerging artistic talent "in harmony with the natural surroundings." He built some of Sundance's buildings with his own hands; that's commitment. His "passion and stubbornness for the arts persevered" against considerable early adversities. Today, Sundance and especially its Film Festival are world renowned and respected.

Dr. Mendelsohn and his team convincingly demonstrate why the University of Texas M.D. Anderson Cancer Center is the world's leader in cancer treatment and research. Their long-term dedication to "making cancer history" was evident as they reviewed genetic susceptibility to cancer, gene replacement therapy, and other research to prevent and treat cancer, which are very promising.

As one of the major figures in public life during the latter part of the 20th century, former President Bush's remarkable career reflects a continuing commitment to serving the nation: Distinguished Flying Cross for bravery; U.S. representative; GOP party chairman; U.N. Ambassador; CIA chief, and eight years as vice president of the United States. Becoming president was the culmination of a career dedicated to public service.

Each of these outstanding people had complex circumstances in their individual lives that helped shape them. Nonetheless, each possessed a clarity of purpose and direction regarding their lives and then had the courage to live that dream, not just dream it.

The key to Napoleon's successful leadership during the last century was summarized by a military writer of this time, "to concentrate . . . force as much as possible at the point where the decisive blows are to be struck." He could well be describing the battlefield of life for all of us.

President George H. W. Bush
AP/WIDE WORLD PHOTOS.

Actor Robert Redford
AP/WIDE WORLD PHOTOS.

A Great Lady Advises: Don't Be Afraid To Try

(Published December 12, 1998)

"Loving and being loved, and having someone with whom to share, is what life is really all about. When you reach my age, you will understand that."

"Learn something else from my experience. I have no regrets about what I have done; I regret what I did not do."

These thoughts were my mother's succinct gift of wisdom and insight at a celebration in honor of her 80th birthday last week. From someone who always seems so energetic, positive, capable, and open to new experiences, it is difficult to imagine what she had wanted to do, and did not do.

The guidance to her children to lead our lives so that we do not regret later not ever attempting to fulfill dreams, or to pursue personal goals, is applicable to all of us.

Many people lead lives of silent frustration, wherein they consider inspiring choices, but do not take action. From some, specific circumstances and responsibilities, such as taking care of children or ill family members, require commitments that preclude other pursuits for a time. Many people, however, hold back, less from external conditions than from self-imposed limitations rooted in lack of confidence, fear of failure, or just inertia.

Increasing numbers of people are overcoming these inhibitions and are thinking and acting individually and independently; they are pursuing their passion and "going for it."

Some change careers; some enter public service. Others return to school to learn previously unexplored subjects. Some travel extensively and others discover spirituality. Some try to climb mountains while others watch more sunsets. The specific activity will vary with each person. Some think that such decisions should be taken by those who are young; in fact, one can follow a road not previously taken at any age.

Virtually all aspects of life may be positively impacted by taking strong action related to what you are strongly committed to - relationships, education, career, personal interests and hobbies, or contributing to a worthy cause. Transition and change are part of life's journey; pursuing an objective about which one truly cares may be the most personally rewarding possible change.

One need not pursue only that which is popular and accepted at a given time. Not too long ago, a concentration on sports or spending time in a garage or basement experimenting with unproven, unaccepted technology was not considered good character preparation. Nonetheless, outstanding accomplishments were achieved by those who followed their passions in these areas, i.e., Michael Jordan, Bill Gates, and Michael Dell.

Regardless of possible eventual success, there is considerable satisfaction in attempting to realize your dream. Without trying, one may spend a lifetime wondering "what if?"

My mother's words, along with the following, may be helpful in thinking about our own lives:

"Do not follow where the path may lead. Go, instead, where there is no path and leave a trail."

- Anonymous

Bertha Klein

Jay Pritzker Was An Extraordinary Man

(Published February 20, 1999)

By any measure, Jay Pritzker led an extraordinary life. He was an exceptionally capable, creative, and gifted person; he died in his hometown of Chicago four weeks ago this morning.

While he was admired in U.S. and international business circles, and beloved by those who knew him, he was virtually unknown to the public. In an age of celebrity and self-promotion, he maintained an unassuming modesty and a penchant for no personal publicity.

His tremendous accomplishments and personal strengths qualify this essentially private person to be a true legend of his time. Warren Buffett heralded Jay as "brilliant" in a letter to his Berkshire Hathaway shareholders and spoke of him as one of the smartest investors that he has ever known. The *Chicago Tribune* described Jay as "Chicago's leading philanthropist."

Jay was a visionary; he started the Hyatt hotel chain on the premise that travelling business people would want to stay at a quality hotel near an airport. Hyatt, which has 182 hotels, with 34 under construction, is a private company owned by his family. He was an outstanding dealmaker who, along with his brother, built a significant private company in manufacturing and industry. At different times, he held substantial interests in companies ranging from Ticketmaster, McCall's magazine, and American Medical International to countless others. He was doing leveraged buyouts decades before they became popular.

He created the Pritzker Architectural Prize which is recognized around the world as the Nobel of its field. Its first recipient was Philip Johnson, who designed our Art Museum of South Texas.

Jay was among the earliest Americans to go global with his business and personal interests many years ago. He was continually curious and enjoyed pursuing the unknown. The purpose of life for him was life itself and activity;

he believed that unless you were moving forward, you were falling behind. He had the spirit of someone who was forever young - with limitless possibilities.

One of his many distinguishing personal qualities was a warm personal style - with a wonderful sense of humor. He was very comfortable with himself - with who and what he was. He was focused, hard-working and had the highest standards of integrity and loyalty. He was straightforward and friendly. He was equally at ease as a guest in the White House or a small cabin.

I was privileged to know Jay as a mentor, friend, and partner for 30 years. We were so close at one time that he referred to himself as my Uncle Jay. The many trips that we took together to Europe, when he was expanding Hyatt internationally and I was developing a Wall Street firm's foreign investment banking business, were especially memorable. We spoke and laughed about those times often, including shortly before his death.

When the definitive history of the 20th century is written and its greatest business leaders and innovators recognized, Jay Pritzker will be where he usually could be found--at or near the top and winning. He will be remembered both for what he accomplished and for the family members to whom he entrusted the opportunity and responsibility to carry on his family's name and interests well into the next century.

Jay A. Pritzker

Dr. Saul Grossman, A Gifted Man, Will Be Missed

(Published August 28, 1999)

Dr. Saul Grossman was a remarkable, wonderful person and a gifted physician. His death at age 88 earlier this month concluded a full life of meaning and purpose.

Saul, who was my father-in-law, was among the last of what has been appropriately described as America's "greatest generation." They were essentially defined by the Depression and World War II and then spent the rest of their lives building this country and enhancing life in their communities. They believed in service to others, duty, hard work, perseverance, honor, courage, and patriotism.

Saul devoted most of his life to loving and caring for his family and friends (many of whom were also patients), to continuing to study and learn, to the practice of medicine, and to a deep commitment to Corpus Christi and the surrounding area and the people therein. For him, there was no place like this part of South Texas.

He was the youngest of eleven children who emigrated to Corpus Christi from Russia in the early 1900's with their mother Rebecca. Their family home is in Heritage Park. The plaque placed in front of it by the Texas Historical Commission reads, "(Mrs. Grossman's) descendents in Corpus Christi were outstanding leaders in business, medicine, law, politics, and religious affairs." Saul was one of four "leaders in...medicine" who were Grossman family members and doctors in the Coastal Bend during most of the 20th century.

Saul practiced medicine in Corpus Christi for 65 years. He prevailed over adversity a number of times, including when he arrived in this state at age 9 unable to speak English. He went on to become one of the youngest ever to graduate from the University of Texas Medical School and to being recently recognized as the longest practicing physician at Christus Spohn Hospital. He had enormous energy and vitality and actively practiced medicine until the day before he died. He was a warm and wise man with an educated intellect combined with common sense and good judgment.

In a eulogy at a standing-room-only funeral service, Saul was compared with the great Medieval physician and philosopher, Maimonides. Both were exceptional doctors who were especially compassionate and genuinely concerned about their patients.

Saul had an enormous capacity for caring; he had an encyclopedic heart as well as mind. He was never too busy, too tired, or too self-absorbed to respond to the call of someone who needed him, or to offer advice. He was also never too serious to tell or hear a good joke, or find humor and enjoyment in life.

His kindness, caring, and love were reciprocated by many people as reflected in the tremendous outpouring of expressions of love and loss at his death; they included the following:

"Saul is already caring for the Lord, treating his illnesses, so that he can watch over me as I try to mold and shape my life to be half the person that Saul was in his lifetime. I loved him dearly and shall miss him until the day that I die."

"A terrific man, excellent physician, and, as a great role model, was deeply loved and will be deeply missed." (from a doctor)

"His strong ethical standards, sense of community service, his love of family, friends, and country will inspire many generations in the future."

Dr. Saul Grossman

Section IX

Introduction Of Lady Margaret Thatcher, Keynote Speaker At The Spohn-South Texas Lyceum Dinner

Introduction Of Lady Margaret Thatcher, Keynote Speaker At The Spohn-South Texas Lyceum Dinner

By Melvyn N. Klein

February 19, 1998

Please take a moment to look at your family members and friends sitting with you — for when you see each other in the months and years to come, you will recall this evening. You will remember it because our distinguished guest speaker, Lady Margaret Thatcher, is one of the world's most admired and best respected true leaders of our time. In fact, when the definitive history of the 20th century is written, it will undoubtedly portray two great struggles - one between freedom and democracy vs. tyranny and communism and the other struggle between free and open markets vs. closed or government-controlled economies. Lady Thatcher is a true hero in the still unfinished, but continuing triumph of freedom and free markets throughout the world.

Lady Thatcher rose to her position from modest circumstances as the daughter of a grocer active in local politics to graduate from Oxford University. She became a research chemist and read law in her spare time. She was called to the Bar and became a barrister, specializing in taxation law.

Her career in public office began in 1959 when she was elected to the House of Commons as Member for Finchley. For the next 20 years, she held a number of significant governmental and political positions, including Secretary of State for Education and Science, member of the Shadow Cabinet and Opposition front bench spokesman on the environment and Treasury. She became the Leader of the Conservative Party and thus Leader of the Opposition in 1975.

On May 4, 1979, she became the first female Prime Minister in Britain's history following the Conservative success in the General Election the day before. She was the only Prime Minister this century to contest successfully three consecutive general elections. She served 11½ consecutive years as Prime Minister, longest since the Napoleonic Wars - almost 200 years ago.

She became Prime Minister during a time of economic crisis in Britain. Lady Thatcher effected significant change and rejuvenation in her country. She revitalized the British economy by reducing the economic role of government and emphasizing individual initiative and a strong free market economy. London maintained its role as a leading world center of finance. She privatized previous government monopolies such as British Airways, telephone service, and distribution of gas and water. She maintained close ties with the United States and was a staunch ally.

She resigned as Prime Minister on November 28, 1990. In 1992, she was elevated to the House of Lords to become Baroness Thatcher of Kesteven. She has written two excellent books *The Downing Street Years* and *The Path to Power.*

As is evident tonight by the number of people here, Lady Thatcher is a living legend both for what she has done and for who she is - she is a moral leader of substance and strength, a person with deep commitment to Judaic-Christian values; a leader who never used opinion polls to guide her where to lead. She is a tour de force who has consistently acted with courage, with great competence, with dignity, and with honor.

Ladies and Gentlemen ... Lady Margaret Thatcher.